A Balanced Life

Living the Hula Hoop Principle

A Balanced Life

Living the Hula Hoop Principle

Dr. Charles B. Beckert & Dr. Derry L. Brinley

CFI
Springville, Utah

ISBN 13: 978-1-55517-943-4
ISBN 10: 1-55517-943-6

Published by CFI, an imprint of Cedar Fort, Inc., 2373 W. 700 S., Springville, UT, 84663
Distributed by Cedar Fort, Inc., www.cedarfort.com

LIBRARY OF CONGRESS CATALOGING-IN-PUBLICATION DATA

Beckert, Charles B.
A balanced life / by Charles B. Beckert and Derry L. Brinley.
p. cm.
Includes bibliographical references and index.
ISBN 1-55517-943-6 (alk. paper)
1. Success. 2. Conduct of life. 3. Christian life--Mormon authors. I. Brinley, Derry L. II. Title.

BJ1611.2.B42 2006
170'.44--dc22

2006018832

Cover design by Nicole Williams
Cover design © 2006 by Lyle Mortimer
Typeset by Annaliese Cox

Printed in the United States of America

10   9   8   7   6   5   4   3   2   1

Printed on acid-free paper

Table of Contents

Preface

Go ahead and ask. What do a hula hoop and a happy person have in common? This is a legitimate question, one we would like to answer it in the pages of this book.

In a nutshell, we believe that many of the principles that allow us to keep a hoop twirling around our waists rather than falling to our ankles can also assist us in our pursuit of happiness and contentment in life. The overriding principle has to do with establishing and maintaining balance, which, when accompanied by specific skills, keeps the hula hoop around our waists (where it belongs) and our lives in harmony.

These specific skills include five "C's": coordination (elements working together in harmony), concentration (attention, awareness, and focus), control (choice and power over responses), cadence (rhythm, pace, and tempo), and continuous motion (constant and unrelenting patience and endurance). Put them together in the appropriate mix, and you have balance. And when you have balance you have happiness.

In other words, successful hula hooping and experiencing happiness can be achieved through establishing and maintaining balance.

To explain this concept more fully, we relate a true story shared by Chris, who added exciting insights to this book. Chris wrote: "When I was young, my brother, sister, and I were pretty good at the hula hoop. In fact, we could balance them around our hips and our arms at the same time. It was fun. A couple of years ago, my kids wanted me to try hula hooping. I said, 'No problem. Move over and watch a pro do this.' Well, sadly, I couldn't do it. For whatever reason, I had lost the balance and coordination I had had as a child. Or at least I thought I had. However, it only took me a few tries and several rotations before I started to get the hang of it again. It only took a few minutes with my kids watching and playing with them to find myself 'balanced' again, inside and out. I was hula hooping with the best of them."

Our point is that Chris's rediscovery of the skills needed to twirl a hula hoop allowed him to also rediscover the much-sought-after balance. This is how many of us face life. We may think we have lost something we once had, or we may feel a little embarrassed in front of others when we fail, but once we make the necessary adjustments we again can experience success.

We do not intend to imply that, in order to experience balance in life, we have to be an expert hula hooper! Rather, we want our readers to understand that in any aspect of life, be it hula hooping, working in our chosen occupation, or getting along in our families, similar principles can assist us in our endeavors. To be positively happy in life, we must learn to establish and maintain balance. Happy hula hooping to you all!

Acknowledgments

We express appreciation to our families, especially our wives, Olga and Carol, for their continued help and support during the writing of this manuscript. It has not always been easy for them. We are also indebted and grateful to the mentors who tutored and trained us. We add our sincere gratitude to the many patients and clients who have shared with us their lives and have taught us so much. May they live in balance and enjoy personal peace and harmony.

Our gratitude is also extended in full measure to the masterful editing work of Lisa McMullin who brought order from chaos.

We are also very thankful for the blessings of a loving Heavenly Father who makes all things possible and who loves His children eternally.

Introduction

Whether we hear it in the valedictorian's speech, the wish of the beauty pageant contestant, or the words that escape the lips of the young child, we are impressed with the common petition for *peace*. We all want to live peaceful lives in a peaceful world. But what many of us do not realize is that the peace we seek—both individual peace and world peace—begins with us.

A father was watching his eight-year-old son while his wife was away. It was Saturday afternoon, and the father was involved in an important football game on television. The young boy wanted his father to spend time with him, and he kept trying to get his father's attention.

The father came up with what he thought was an ingenious plan. He located a large map of the world in the newspaper and cut it into many small pieces. Handing the puzzle pieces to his son, the father instructed the boy to put the map of the world together. "Come get me when you're done," the father said, "and then we'll spend the rest of the afternoon together."

The father was confident the task would keep the boy occupied long enough for him to watch the rest of the game. About twenty minutes later, however, his young son bounded in the room, announcing that he'd completed the assignment.

The father checked, and sure enough, the world was together. "How did you put the puzzle together so quickly?" he asked his son.

"On the other side of the world map was a picture of a little boy," his son answered with a smile. "I put the boy together, and the world took care of itself."

Like the boy in the story, we must put the pieces of our lives together and find a harmonious balance before we can experience first personal peace and then, ideally, world peace.

The terrorist attack on the World Trade Center on September 11, 2001, was certainly not a step toward world peace, yet many people consider it a turning point in their lives. Thousands were directly affected, while millions more were indirectly affected. The suddenness and scope of the experience pushed many off balance and out of step with life. Many found themselves rethinking and reevaluating their personal values. What seemed vitally important prior to the attack no longer seemed as significant.

For example, as a whole, society's thoughts and attitudes toward patriotism were measurably heightened as we began to view our personal freedom with a deeper respect. At the same time, our feelings of security and fearlessness became less evident. Personal balance was upset, and many continue to stumble as they strive to come to grips with this attack. We needed to reassess our basic values and redirect our lives if we were to again feel in balance.

Along with this terrible experience came a realization about what in life was of *real value.* Temporal and worldly concerns no longer ranked as our most important priorities. We learned that in a fleeting moment temporal things could be lost. The less tangible elements, the weightier matters, moved to the top of our lists.

Our challenge is to achieve and maintain balance in our lives even though we are bombarded with demands on every side. Many important "things" bid for our limited time and energy, things that fill our plates to overflowing. The most demanding aspects of our daily life include spouse, family, church, work, school, community, friends, and personal interests. For most of us, life requires a monumental juggling act.

This vital tenet of balance is essential to the principle of hula hooping. We can be taught the intricacies and techniques of the hula hoop by others, yet ultimately each of us must develop our own style and preferences that fit our personal beliefs, situations, and current attitude. Each of us must identify, understand, and then work toward the goal of keeping the hula hoop in balanced motion. As we do so, we will receive the personal reward of our efforts—joy, peace, and satisfaction of a balanced life! Thus, all the learning, aggravation, practice, and effort will have been worth it.

M. Russell Ballard described this circumstance in these words: "Coping with the complex and diverse challenges of everyday life, which is not an easy task, can upset the balance and harmony we seek. Many good people who really care a lot are trying very hard to maintain balance, but they sometimes feel overwhelmed and defeated."[1]

As psychotherapists, we spend the bulk of our professional lives with emotionally healthy people whose lives are temporarily out of balance. These individuals are confused, frustrated, and *not* experiencing peace and harmony in their lives. Therapy represents a constructive and positive way to assist people in rediscovering and reinstating balance in their lives. We believe an individual can reach the goal of balance through an appropriate application of the hula hoop principles presented in this book combined with the five "C" skills (coordination, concentration, control, cadence, and continuous motion).

In the writing of this book, we draw heavily upon what we have learned from the experiences of people we have known as clients and patients over the years. All the case studies shared in this book are based on true stories with the necessary alteration of personal information to protect the privacy of those who lived them.

It is not our intent or ability to provide all things to all people, but we can offer a variety of ideas from which you can choose to help bring balance back into your lives.

We hope this book will provide a message of hope and happiness to you, and we expect the concepts and strategies we share to lift spirits and instill confidence in the hearts of any who sense their lives to be out of balance.

We wish you good reading.

Dr. Beckert and Dr. Brinley

––––––––––

Note

1. M. Russell Ballard, "Keeping Life's Demands in Balance," *Ensign*, May 1987, 13.

Principles Overview

The first section of this book discusses the basic concept of balance, what it is, and why it is important to attain and maintain. Comparisons are provided to demonstrate how a balanced person and an unbalanced individual might encounter and respond to some of the more common challenges of life.

Section two discusses the process of change and suggests an order of steps or phases for this process. The steps identified are: recognize the feelings of imbalance, accept our condition, understand the causes of our imbalance, become aware of how far we have strayed to the left or to the right, define our goal for balance, develop the motivation to make necessary changes, take action toward our goal, invite and accept feedback to maintain focus and direction, adjust as needed, and finally, enjoy the resulting balance in our lives.

The third section identifies several attitudes and behaviors which act as barriers, inhibiting and blocking our balance. We present actual case scenarios to illustrate how these barriers work to create and maintain the frustration and confusion so many experience. In addition, you will have opportunity to evaluate where you stand in relationship to each barrier. The numbers provided at the conclusion of many of the case studies can direct the reader to specific strategies or techniques we have found helpful in these and similar situations. These strategies make up the content of section four of the book and are numbered to help the reader locate any in which they have specific interest.

The fourth section contains the "nuts and bolts" of this book. It is a section on change, and change is something each of us must experience if we want to find ourselves in better balance. We present numerous general and specific strategies, designed to overcome the barriers and help you to more effectively achieve and maintain balance. These strategies which have been used with hundreds of our clients and patients and have proven helpful in many instances, are worthy of discussion and application. You could select any number of them from this menu to reestablish the peace and harmony you desire.

The fifth and final section of this book serves as a declaration of hope and success. We can succeed and find happiness, contentment, and fulfillment in the process of personal growth. The magic is to achieve and maintain balance. When in balance we can enjoy peace and harmony. You and I can make it! That is our promise!

Section I
About Balance

Balance in Life

We choose to look at balance in two ways. First, we see balance as representing personal attitudes and behaviors that are in the middle of the road rather than being too extreme in any given area. Extremes are prime culprits in pushing individuals off balance. We also view balance in a social manner and equate it with being at peace and in harmony with all aspects of our lives: personal, social, and spiritual.

In our experience, individuals seek counseling because they feel out of balance in one or more of these areas:

- Their relationship with their Creator
- What is going on within their own lives
- Their relationships with family members, friends, and associates
- How they function in their familial, occupational, and social environments

The degree of unbalance varies by how far from center people feel they are.

We believe we are each individually responsible for the personal balance or unbalance we experience. We are where we are as a result of decisions we have made and things we have done. Because the unbalance we are sensing is a consequence of our own attitudes and actions, we have the capacity to regain our balance. It is within our power to make choices that allow us to achieve balance and enjoy peace and harmony.

For example, if we choose a path that increases the distance between us and our desired goal, we increase the likelihood of going out of balance. On the other hand, if we elect to do things in line with our ideals, we will enjoy closer harmony within ourselves, and with the people around us.

The five key skills necessary for successful hula hooping—coordination, concentration, control, cadence, and continuous motion—can work equally as effectively when it comes to maintaining balance in our lives.

- Coordination of the different and demanding areas of our lives allows us to experience harmony and peace in our world.
- Concentration focuses our attention and awareness on the task at hand without a total disregard for other significant elements.
- Maintaining personal control of our own thoughts, feelings, and actions prevents us from expending our energies in areas that are outside of our direct influence.
- Demonstrating an appropriate cadence encourages us to stay within our limits and move gradually and surely toward our goal.
- The final skill, continuous motion, keeps us moving, so we do not encounter "dead times."

Challenging Philosophies of Our Day

Many pressures and challenges push us off center and out of balance. We have noticed, however, that some pressures and challenges appear with such frequency and regularity that they have become philosophies by which many people live. These philosophies make it difficult to stay in the middle of the road because they push us to one extreme or the other. At times their influence is strong enough to force us completely off the road.

How many people do you know who embrace the "buy now, pay later" philosophy? Many of these people will not sense their unbalance and discomfort until the "later" catches up with them.

Another modern philosophy is that of instant gratification or the "quick fix." Those who follow this philosophy believe life is like the television programs that solve sticky issues in a matter of minutes. Similarly, our age seems to be one of disposability; if something fails to work, rather than having it repaired, we throw it out and purchase a new one. This is sadly true even with our interpersonal relationships.

Have you ever wondered how many people have been thrown off balance in their attempt to embrace the philosophy of "equality equals sameness"? Failure to make allowances for individual differences and attempting to treat everyone exactly the same guarantees unnecessary challenges and difficulties.

Blaming others for our problems and refusing to accept personal responsibility is another philosophy of our day that creates discomfort rather than peace. A recent news article reported that a woman was suing a fast food restaurant because she had spilled hot coffee on her lap while climbing into her car; she blamed the restaurant because the coffee she had purchased was too hot. And a man has sued several fast food restaurants, maintaining that his morbid obesity was the fault of their products rather than his addiction to fast food and inability to eat less.

One additional imbalancing philosophy suggests that we should live today as if there were no tomorrow—*carpe diem* taken to extremes. Few people wake up from such an adventure feeling in balance with life. Either the hula hoop is spinning so fast it is out of control, or it has slowed to the point that it falls to the ground.

Internals versus Externals

One common characteristic of unbalanced individuals is their reliance on the external rather than the internal parts of their lives. These people are more concerned about wealth, beauty, fame, or what others think of them than they are about whether they are kind, courteous, respectful, honest, and loving. These personal characteristics represent how we look on the inside. People who are more concerned about what they are on the inside than how they appear on the outside generally experience better balance in life.

This poem emphasizes the importance of these internal aspects.

My Mother Says

My mother says she doesn't care about the color of my hair,
Or if my eyes are blue or brown, or if my nose turns up or down.
My mother says these things don't matter.
My mother says she doesn't care if I'm dark or if I'm fair
If I'm thin or if I'm fat, she doesn't fret o'er things like that.
My mother says these things don't matter.
But if I cheat or tell a lie, or do mean things and make folks cry,

If I'm rude and impolite and do not try to do what's right–
Then these things really matter.
It isn't looks that make one great, it's character that seals our fate.
It's what's within our hearts you see that makes or mars our destiny.
And that's what really matters.[1]

Our Friends and Our Balance

Balance is easier to maintain when we are friends with ourselves and have friends outside of ourselves. Being around people who care about us helps us maintain a sense of well-being and balance. Perhaps you've heard the slogan that "friends don't let friends drive drunk." It is just as true that "friends don't let friends get too far off balance."

A good friend can do much to help us stay on course and in balance. Picture yourself walking on top of a single railroad rail. How far do you suppose you could walk without losing balance and stepping on the ground? Obviously, the distance would depend on your ability to perform this action.

Now, picture yourself walking along a railroad tie, but now you're holding hands with a friend, who is walking alongside you on a parallel railroad tie. When you have each other to lean on, balancing becomes much easier.

The following are valuable characteristics that can help you identify a true friend—one that you can rely on to help you keep your balance:

- A true friend is someone with whom you can share your innermost thoughts without fear of reprisal.
- A true friend is someone you can trust to keep a confidence.
- A true friend is someone who is always there for you.
- A true friend is someone who knows what you need to hear and is willing to share it with you.
- A true friend is someone who wants to help you.
- A true friend is someone who does not expect or desire compensation for what he does.
- A true friend is someone who knows all about you and values your friendship anyway.
- A true friend is someone who is a friend through the bad times as well as the good.

- A true friend is someone who loves you enough to tell you when you are wrong.
- A true friend is someone who stands up for you and defends your reputation.

In and out of Balance

CB was reading an application submitted by a young woman who wanted to volunteer her time and energies to a cause involving "special" children, as she called them. In the comment section of the application, she wrote: "The reason I would like to work with special children is because I am one."

CB's heart was touched by her recognition of not only what she wanted to do but also of whom she was and what she was capable of doing. This young woman was blessed because she recognized who and where she was. Many of us are not able to do this. And if we don't know where we are, we certainly can't know how to get where we would like to be.

This problem is common among those seeking our help. They recognize something is not right in their lives, but they are generally at a loss as to what that something might be or how to fix it.

Below are five scenarios describing common situations. These scenarios describe both balanced and unbalanced reactions.

Scenario 1: Driver A is driving along, minding his own business but driving a bit under the posted speed limit. Driver B is right on his tail, feeling frustrated because he is unable to pass. Unless there is an extreme emergency, a balanced Driver B will remain a safe distance behind the vehicle A, anxiously waiting for an appropriate opportunity to pass. On the other hand, if Driver B is unbalanced, he might tailgate, honk the horn continuously, flash his lights in the rear view mirror, or even exhibit specific hand gestures designed to irritate and agitate other drivers. When the opportunity to pass finally comes, unbalanced Driver B may swing in front of Driver A quickly, forcing Driver A to apply his brakes to avoid an accident. Once Driver B has made his move, the focus is now on the personal balance of the driver in car A. How might he react? If Driver A is in balance, he will continue to drive, allowing Driver B to proceed on his way. If, however, Driver A is not in balance; he might make even poorer choices than did Driver B, weaving and chasing Driver B through traffic or something as equally dangerous.

Scenario 2: This example was written by Sydney J. Harris for the *Chicago Daily News*. He wrote:

> *I walked with my friend, a Quaker, to the newsstand the other night and he bought a paper, thanking the newsman politely. The newsman didn't even acknowledge it.*
>
> *"A sullen fellow, isn't he?" I commented.*
>
> *"Oh, he's that way every night," shrugged my friend.*
>
> *"Then why do you continue to be so polite to him?" I asked.*
>
> *"Why not?" inquired my friend. "Why should I let him decide how I'm going to act?"*[2]

The Quaker gentleman was certainly in balance as he responded to the rude newspaperman. An unbalanced individual would most likely have returned rudeness for rudeness or perhaps walked away without the paper he wanted to read.

Scenario 3: A family is going on vacation. Sometimes traveling can be nerve-racking, especially for parents. A balanced parent will enjoy the journey as well as the destination. Squabbles between family members are recognized—even expected—and judiciously resolved without a loss of control. Having a good time is more important than getting there as quickly as possible. The atmosphere in the vehicle is light and cheerful, filled with positive communication and interesting activities.

On the other hand, an unbalanced parent may drive like a maniac to arrive regardless of anyone's discomfort. He may be so on edge that the slightest wrinkle in the family fabric turns into a gigantic tear. Aggressive driving, abusive language, and unrealistic expectations are all symptomatic of this unbalance. And as a result, the rest of the family is unhappy.

Scenario 4: When it comes to finances, both Person A and Person B are unbalanced. Person A is frugal to the point of starvation, literally and figuratively. Every penny is accounted for. Small extras like eating out occasionally or buying an ice cream cone after a baseball game are unnecessary expenditures. On the flip side of the coin, Person B demonstrates little or no regard for money and has no concept of managing it. He owes $30,000 on his credit cards and can't stop spending. He and his wife fight about finances almost daily. She wants a divorce; he is miserable.

While most couples find it necessary to make continual adjustments with their family finances, those who are balanced do so without argument and fanfare. Both partners understand the attitudes and behaviors of one another, and each avoids extreme frugality as well as excessive spending.

Scenario 5: Our final scenario features a recent news story about a Little League baseball game. The batter slashed the ball into the gap between left and center field. The center fielder missed the ball (not uncommon in Little League competition) and had to chase it to the fence. The batter rounded first base and kept running, rounding second base just as the fielder threw the ball toward the infield.

The third baseman was young and small and didn't know where to stand, so he stood right on top of the base. The hitter was older and significantly bigger than the third baseman and was determined to make it to the bag safely. The ball arrived at the base a second or so before the runner. The tag out seemed certain to everyone but the larger boy who saw the smaller boy standing in the base path just in front of the bag. The hitter lowered his shoulder and ran right into the third baseman, knocking him head over heels. The ball squirted out of his glove and fell to the ground. The umpire called the runner safe as the poor little third baseman lay motionless about ten feet away.

The unbalanced father of the third baseman did not care that his son was standing right in the path of the hitter, and the father of the runner did not care that his son was twice the size of the third baseman. The first father showed little concern for his son's condition and began screaming and hollering at the hitter. He attempted to attack the hitter for what he had done.

The hitter's unbalanced father did not care that his son was twice the size of the third baseman, and when the third baseman's father attempted to attack his son, he lunged for the other father. The end result was a horrific fight between the two fathers, which eventually ended in the death of one of the fathers.

Had the father of the third baseman been in balance and accepted his son's part of the problem, he would have exerted his energies in helping his son.

Had the hitter's father been balanced, he would not have attacked the unbalanced father but rather pulled him off his son and allowed him to cool off.

Maintaining balance is a vital key to successfully negotiating life's trials and tribulations. Overreacting or underreacting—in other words, being out of balance—when we face challenging situations will most assuredly create larger problems than those we originally faced. We need to maintain personal balance.

Not unlike trying to keep our hula hoop from dropping, maintaining balance is a common problem especially during the day-to-day struggles we all confront. During these times, we often forget what is most important to us. In the heat of the battle, we frequently focus on our current situation or task, concentrating on getting through our day or the week. Many of us feel that if we can only get through this week of recitals or the upcoming wedding, or whatever, life will return to normal. Then we will be able to slow down, and all will be well.

Unfortunately, this never appears to happen. During our busy lives, full of self-imposed nearsightedness, we often lost sight of our purpose in life and what our highest priorities and goals are. In other words, we are so worried about each small element of hula hooping, we forget that it is the coordination of several skills that keeps the hoop spinning.

In order to make the necessary changes, we must recognize that we may be out of balance and then pursue the necessary transformations to return our lives to harmony and balance. As we approach perfect balance, we can enjoy that which we all seek: peace, harmony, and contentment.

These don't come without effort or cost, but they are within reach of anyone who follows the basic rules of balance.

Middle of the Road

As mental health professionals, we see people who struggle daily with many types of difficulties. Many do not understand the primary cause of their troubles. They wonder why they must struggle and suffer so much. Some even wonder if God is really there, and if so, does He care about them.

If we were to generalize the problems our patients bring to us, we would summarize their discomfort as a struggle for balance. They feel drawn this way and that by too many obligations and pressures, yet they yearn for peace and harmony in their lives. Their desire is to maintain efficiency and balance with *all* the demands of life and to complete each task flawlessly.

Unfortunately, the total realization of this expectation is impossible. Almost without exception, those we see in our office are out of balance. Never does someone come into our office and tell us that everything in her life is exactly the way she wants it, including a marriage that is wonderful, children who are doing well, plenty of good friends, and a gratifying and fulfilling job.

Our clientele consists of those who are out of balance and who are experiencing frustrations and confusion. Their hula hoops are slipping because they have strayed either too far to the right or too far to the left of the midline.

Illustrated below is a visual illustration we use in the office to demonstrate our point:

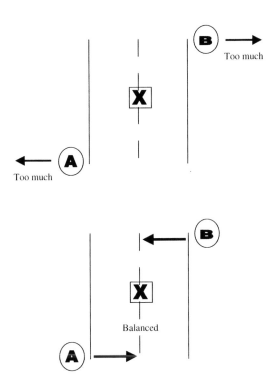

As you can see, individual X is in the center or middle of the road. Individuals who manage to handle life in this position do relatively well. However, individuals A and B are at extremes and are generally out of balance. We work to help individual A move to the right, closer to the middle. We also want to help individual B move to the left, closer to the middle.

The changes we suggest take time, effort, and consistency, but the rewards are extremely worthwhile. People with extreme unbalances are not unintelligent, but they frequently lose focus and thus their balance in life. They have lost their direction and need to be shown how to regain balance by eliminating negative thoughts and detrimental behaviors.

Interestingly, many of these individuals have been rewarded in the past for unhealthy behaviors. If those rewards continue, these people will be unable to see that they have moved too far left or too far right.

For example, Gloria was losing her family because she couldn't control her temper. Her husband could no longer tolerate her anger. Her children had little or no respect for her and either ignored or disobeyed her. If things didn't go the way she felt they should go, she would yell, swear, and throw and break things. Her fits continued until she felt better or got her way.

She entered counseling seeking the "secrets" to happiness and keeping her family. One major hurdle for her was to understand that she was looking outside herself for the solution; she had to understand that *she* was at the root of her own problems. More often than not, we are our own worst enemies.

During counseling, we discovered that, as a child, when Gloria didn't get her way, she threw a fit and eventually her wants and needs were granted. It is a no-brainer to figure out that when we are rewarded for what we do, we do it more often. That's human nature. Unfortunately, Gloria had been rewarded for her angry behavior her entire life, and now at age forty-five, her world was crumbling around her and she wondered why.

To change, Gloria first had to recognize that her own behavior was the root of the problem. She could not blame her husband or her children. Second, she needed to be motivated to change, not just change until things were less bad, but change until things became good. Many people change until things are getting better, and then they stop, much like people who take their prescribed antibiotics until they feel better and then stop, not completing the full treatment.

Third, Gloria had to continue to do things differently for a real and permanent change to occur. In training, we learned a simple yet profound lesson: If nothing changes, nothing will change. This may sound trite or overly simplistic, but we see many who do not comprehend and internalize this powerful lesson.

Finally, Gloria and her family had to develop patience and allow time for the changes to occur. Her thoughts and behaviors had developed over many years and could not be expected to change overnight. It takes time and tremendous effort to bring ourselves back into balance.

Earlier, we mentioned Chris, who thought it would be simple to pick up hula hooping where he left off, even though he had not hula hooped for a long time. To his dismay, Chris had to relearn some of the necessary skills he had mastered years before. Once he recognized what was not working, he found a way to make adjustments that enabled him to regain his mastery of the hoop.

Notes

1. The Idea Door, "My Mother Says," http://www.theideadoor.com/integrity.htm (accessed October 30, 2006).

2. Sterling W. Sill, *Principles, Promises, and Powers* (Salt Lake City: Deseret Book, 1973), 34.

Section II
A Process of Change

Life in mortality is a dynamic, ever-changing, ever-growing experience—a period of continuous adjustments as we confront various life events. Life contains events, stages, and phases. And if we wait long enough, something new occurs in our lives, something that may require an adjustment, if not a significant change in attitude and behavior.

Franklin D. Richards stated, "We are living in a period of social adjustments and constant changes and a time of unprecedented growth and development: the age of the jet airplane, the computer, and the communications satellite. As we look at the world situation today, I feel that a large percentage of the people are seeking a plan of life that will bring them peace, relief from inner tensions, happiness, and growth and development."[1]

We must learn to adjust to life's changes if we are to maintain proper balance, or a condition of peace and harmony within ourselves, between ourselves and those we meet and deal with, and between ourselves and our Maker, depending on our personal belief system.

Rabbi Harold S. Kushner describes this constant challenge as a battle between "our two selves," meaning our public and private selves.[2] This battle is compounded by our struggle to be balanced in our relationships with those around us.

Of course, it is one thing to understand the need for balance and the need to achieve it and quite another to accomplish this awesome but worthwhile task. This section offers suggestions that address the proverbial question: How do I get there from here?

Because each of us is unique and each situation is unlike any other, we have suggested a general process that fits most situations. Some custom fitting and fine tuning may be necessary as you personalize these steps and do what is needed to achieve your personal balance in whatever areas of your life you might select.

This table illustrates the process of change we are presenting, providing a keyword and a question for each step. In addition, we provide a brief description of each step in the changing process—steps that lead us toward more balanced lives.

Keyword	Question to be answered
Recognize	What is it I am sensing that makes me feel uncomfortable?
Accept	Is this really what I am feeling? Yes, it is!
Understanding	What are the characteristics or areas that cause me concern?
Awareness	How far to the left or right have I strayed from balance?
Goal or Desire	Where do I want to be at this time in my life?
Motivation	Why should I seek balance in this particular area at this particular time?
Action	What changes do I need to make to reach an acceptable balance?
Feedback	How will I know when what I hear is in my best interest?
Adjustments	What else needs to be done to enjoy balance?
Enjoy	No question, simply appreciation and gratitude for this feeling of peace.

RECOGNIZE: Sometimes we sense when we are out of balance in an area of life. We feel something is wrong. We are uncomfortable, even if we don't know what the specific problems might be. However, we have found that most of us are so busy doing so many things that we may not pay attention to the messages our mind, heart, or body may be sending.

Not recognizing when we are out of balance is much like driving along a road, unaware that we are heading in the wrong direction. Sometimes we need someone, perhaps a spouse, friend, or child, to tell us we are going the wrong way. Obviously, just because someone suggests we are out of balance doesn't mean we are, but the suggestion should raise a red flag. We should be open to determining for ourselves the validity of the suggestion. Until we realize we are not going where we intended to go, we will never change directions.

ACCEPT: Once we recognize our unbalance, we need to accept it as real. It is one thing to say we are out of balance and another to accept our condition as reality. We may refuse to accept the fact for several reasons. For instance, if we don't know how to get back on track, we may not want to deal with the problems. Or maybe we simply don't like what we see and refuse to take responsibility for it.

It is important to realize that accepting something is more than merely tolerating it. When we accept our condition, we own it, and once we own it, that means we can—and sometimes should—change it.

Another reason for not accepting our circumstances may be personal insecurity and fear; we simply can't cope with being less than perfect. If we refuse to accept what's going on, we don't have to deal with it.

However, simply put, we will not be able to obtain balance until we accept that something is wrong. After all, if there's nothing wrong, there's no reason for us to change. Acceptance of an unbalanced area in our lives is a vital step to change.

UNDERSTAND: Whether in a military battle or an athletic competition, the better we understand our opponent, the greater our chances for success. The same holds true in our quest for balance. The better we understand unbalanced areas of our lives, the easier it will be for us to avoid the behaviors that create that unbalance, and exhibit the behaviors that lead to balance.

Without this understanding, the remaining steps in the process of change make little sense. The book *The Three Infinities*, by Sterling W. Sill, discusses three separate and distinct yet connected concepts: to know, to do, and to be.[3]

First, Sills proposes, we know and understand something, then we do whatever is required to reach success, and then we become whatever it is we are seeking. Any success without understanding what we are doing would be purely accidental and not likely to be repeated.

AWARENESS: This critical step requires introspection on our part along with the courage to accept what we discover. We may not like how far we have strayed from the middle of the road, but mark it we must. We must also know where we are relative to where we would like to be if our desire is to move in a particular direction.

Unless we are honest about where we fit in regards to a particular characteristic, attitude, or behavior, we may not be motivated to make the changes necessary to reach balance. While it seems reasonable that the further we see ourselves from being balanced, the more motivated we might be to make adjustments, we have also learned that when individuals see themselves too far from where they wish to be, their tendency is often to give up and not try at all. Some even reach the point of accepting the unbalance in their lives.

It is important that our placement on the scale is where *we* perceive it to be, regardless of where others might think we are. Although our personal perception may be influenced by others, we must "own" the placement we give ourselves.

This step might be more easily understood if we imagine ourselves walking into a large building that is unfamiliar. Generally when we walk into such a building, a large map shows the various offices and rooms in the building. This map also shows a large "X" and "You are here." Knowing where we are relative to where we would like to go are the two keys necessary to finding our desired destination. The absence of either blocks our progress.

As we determine where we would like to go, we need to be careful not to expect perfection or have unrealistic expectations. Moderation is wise along with gradual movement in the desired direction.

GOAL OR DESIRE: When we understand about extremes in behavior and know where we stand in relationship to them, our next challenge is to determine where we would like to be in terms of our attitudes, thoughts, or actions. We can ask several questions to help us make those determinations. Those questions might include:

- How would I like to feel?
- How would I like to behave?
- What would I like to do?
- How would I like to react?

The more vivid the vision of our desired thoughts and behaviors is, the greater our chances of realizing them.

Once we identify where we are and where we want to go, we need to identify the steps to take to get there; these steps, often called goals, should be reasonable and reachable.

Write your goals down. A written description of a specific goal is more definitive and identifiable than an imagined, verbal, or visualized one. In other words, the more specific our descriptions, the better our chances are of achieving our goals. Questions such as "What will I look like?" or "What will I act like?" or "What will I think?" are invaluable in our quest for balance. Writing the answers to these questions helps crystallize our thoughts and ideas about where we are relative to the peace and harmony we know we will enjoy when we attain balance.

MOTIVATION: There is a story about an elderly custodian of a small town high school who made a lasting impression on many of the students. One of his daily tasks was to clean the chalkboard, which he did very well. However, every day, he left a few letters written in the upper right-hand corner of the board for all the students to read. The letters? YAREELLYGOTTAWANNA.

Most students understood the message the janitor was sending them, and they knew he meant it. His years of experience and contact with thousands of students had taught him that those who got ahead did so because they really wanted to. They knew their desired destination, and they went after it.

Motivation may be the most crucial step in our strategy to reach and maintain balance. If we are not motivated strongly enough, we will not put forth the required effort, and consequently, success will not be ours. Over and over again, we have seen that want power is a greater force than will power.

While teaching a group of adolescents, CB learned something from a teenage girl, who came from a family that was perceived to be rather unique; family members often did things a little differently than might be expected.

One of the assignments was a class presentation, and about three minutes into her presentation, this young lady stopped and said, "Okay, each of you reach under your chair and pick off whatever is stuck there."

CB found himself holding his breath as the students reached under their seats, wondering what they might find. You can imagine his relief when each of them retrieved a small piece of paper, which had been taped to the bottom of the seat. He was even more impressed with the message typed on each slip of paper: *So often we seek a change in our condition when what we really need is a change in our attitude.* Such a simple statement and yet, to this day, CB hasn't forgotten it.

The main point this young woman wanted to make was that changing our attitudes about what is bothering us is often more effective and much easier than trying to change things beyond our control.

As you think about motivation, consider two basic questions:

- What benefits will come to me if I make these changes?
- What problems will I avoid if I achieve the balance I am seeking?

The more specific we are with our answers, the more motivated we will be to accomplish our task.

ACTION: CB generally hands new patients a small card during their initial visits to the office. Their general response may be a giggle or a slight laugh, but eventually they realize how serious he really is! The card reads, "If nothing changes, nothing will change."

Even in its simplicity, this statement is profoundly true. Some people repeat patterns of behavior over and over before they finally give up and realize that what they are doing is not going to work. It seems ludicrous to do the same things in the same way and expect a different result, yet so many of us do it!

If we are to overcome our unbalance and achieve peace and harmony, something has to change. We have to alter our behavior patterns.

To simplify this step, we suggest the following exercise. Write down the final result you would like to achieve, and then write down a few small steps that you feel will lead you to your goal. This is similar to the process you followed when you learned to tie your shoes as a young child, learning several small actions before attaining the final goal.

Change in behavior is brought about by one of the following: 1) we can start to do something we haven't been doing; 2) we can do more of what we're already doing; 3) we can do less of what we're already doing; or 4) we can stop doing something we've been doing.

If we want to change our present position, we must change something. Taking action is a major key—even though it threatens our comfort zone. Any change in behavior involves risk, and some risks are greater than others. However, there is no other way.

Of course, we need to consider potential consequences of our changes in behavior before we make them, but make them we must if we want to experience the peace and harmony that come with balance.

FEEDBACK: Whether we have chosen to begin doing something, to do something more often, to stop doing something, or to do something less often, we need to know if we are coming closer to our goal. Is what we are doing working? There is little sense in continuing our efforts if we aren't being successful. Somehow we need to find out how we are doing.

The process of receiving information about our actions is called feedback. Feedback comes from several sources. Most commonly, we sense it ourselves or gather it from those closest to us. In the case of hula hooping, the hula hoop itself provides the feedback. If it spins appropriately, what we are doing is working. If it begins to fall, we need to change what we are doing or we will lose the hoop.

Because it is often difficult to monitor our own actions, we often rely on responses from others. Typically, the more significant role a particular individual plays in our lives, the more value we give his feedback. For example, feedback from a spouse carries more weight than similar information coming from a stranger.

Feedback often comes to us whether we want it or not. Although feedback provided by others is usually intended to help, there are times when information others share is meant to harm us, or at least make our life a little more uncomfortable.

It is sometimes helpful to differentiate between types of feedback. Generally, people discuss feedback in terms of being positive or negative. In the cybernetic or systems arena, positive feedback maintains the status quo while negative feedback suggests the need for change.

Most people have a difficult time perceiving negative feedback as helpful. After all, they think, negative means bad or harmful. Because of this, we define feedback in three different categories.

Maintaining Feedback is a form of information designed to sustain the current condition. This feedback is usually gratifying; we like to feel we are doing the right things at the appropriate times and in an acceptable manner.

Modifying Feedback suggests that we could or should make changes. Although we often dread this type of feedback and feel judged and criticized by it, the changes suggested may prove helpful to us in our quest for balance.

Motivating Feedback generally consists of encouragement and support toward change rather than criticism and censure; this type of feedback also facilitates movement in the desired direction.

Receiving and accepting feedback requires an open mind and a willingness to listen to our own feelings as well as suggestions from others. Proud individuals are typically not open to suggestions or feedback, while humble people often welcome counsel.

To disallow feedback or pay little attention to it blocks growth and prevents us from enjoying the peace and harmony of balance in our lives.

ADJUSTMENTS: Feedback is of no value unless we act upon it. We all have the right and the obligation to evaluate all feedback we receive. Some feedback may prove beneficial while other information may not be helpful at all. Remember that feedback is only someone's opinion, and we must assess its validity and usability.

ENJOY: When desired changes have been made and we sense balance, peace, and harmony, it is time to enjoy the fruits of our labors! Being in balance is a wonderful feeling, and we have the right to enjoy it as long as possible.

We need to realize, however, that life goes on and that living is a dynamic process. With life's continuous changes will come needs for further adjustments. However, as we progress, the adjustments we make as we respond to appropriate feedback become smaller and smaller.

Interestingly, a major part of our enjoyment will come from knowing we can make necessary adjustments to achieve balance in any area.

It may be helpful to note how the five "C" skills so useful in successful hula hooping apply to the process of change just discussed.

Coordination between ourselves and those around us is critical if we are to hear, accept, and understand any feedback that may suggest we are out of balance in an area of life. There must also be coordination between our thoughts and our actions if positive change is to be realized.

Concentration allows us to focus our attention and energy on the areas of life where balance is being sought. We must remain aware of the goal if we are to reach it successfully.

Control is a key to the entire plan. We must demonstrate personal power over our responses to the challenges we face. We have control only over our own thoughts, feelings, and actions—and we must exercise that control.

Many people try to change too much in too short a time. *Cadence* is crucial in the process of change. Direction is often a better measure of success than speed. Life has rhythm, pace, and tempo, and our efforts in bringing about change should as well.

Continuous motion is an obvious element of any change process. Even when a goal has been reached, continuous effort is generally required to maintain the achieved position or circumstance. Such motion should be purposeful motion and not just movement.

Notes

1. Franklin D. Richards, in Conference Report, April 1970, 11.

2. Harold S. Kushner, *When Bad Things Happen to Good People* (New York: Avon, 1997).

3. Sterling W. Sill, *The Three Infinities* (Salt Lake City: Bookcraft, 1969), 3.

Section III

Character Extremes
That Affect Balance

In our practices, we have identified common personality or character traits; the extremes of these traits produce barriers to peace, harmony, freedom and joy. Understanding these extremes and where they fall on a continuum—either left or right of a balanced approach—helps us identify what we can do in our efforts to achieve balance. We've included a short description, discussed typical behavior associated with the characteristic, and included an actual case study for clarification. Studying these can help us identify what barriers we may be facing and what changes we may need to make.

INFLEXIBLE ⟷ FLEXIBLE

Inflexible
Description:

Rigid individuals are overly focused on rules and regulations in their thoughts and behaviors. They generally have several or all of the following characteristics: They have a pervasive preoccupation with order, rules, perfection, and control. They tend to walk a very straight and narrow path and find it difficult to deviate at all, even when it seems to be in their best interest. Their minds are filled with perfectionistic thoughts that result in strict and rigid behaviors.

These people demand excellence from themselves and those around them. They manifest an "I'll do it because you'll do it wrong" attitude. They seem preoccupied with work and are intolerant of changes. They have the reputation of being rigid, inflexible, stubborn, and hard to get along with. They are overly scrupulous, moralistic, and nonaccepting of anyone who doesn't share their same morals.

They are stingy with their time, money, talents, and energy. Because they believe their way is the only right way, it is difficult for them to let go of control.

Discussion:

These individuals are clear-cut and close-minded in their thinking and behaviors. They take the skill of concentration to an extreme, usually at the expense of balance. They refuse to consider alternatives and/or listen to feedback from others. They perceive the world a certain way and are frustrated when others don't see it the same way.

They believe they know what is best and often personify Proverbs 12:15, which states, "the way of a fool is right in his own eyes." These individuals commonly become angry and frustrated when confronted about their views of rigidity, control, or inflexibility. They may merely redirect the "problem" to others, saying or thinking, "Well, they just don't understand facts or see it clearly, so . . ."

In the workplace, they are often excellent employees. They give more than they are paid to. They are self-motivated; they stay late and never take sick leave or vacation. They are frequently sought by employers for their excessive work ethic, dependability, and high values.

However, because of their rigidity and need for rules and control, they struggle tremendously with relationships. They are so consumed with their own thoughts and behaviors that others find them difficult to be around. Associates, friends, and family don't feel comfortable around them. Those close to inflexible people often say they have to walk on eggshells for fear of becoming the target of anger, judgment, and retaliation.

Many individuals may cling to this extreme trait because they do not see other alternatives. Others may be so fearful of failure and potential negative consequences they are afraid to break out of their comfort zone. Prideful people are almost always inflexible, rigid, and stubborn. Their need for control, which is generally safer and does not allow others the power to hurt them, encourages rigidity in thought and action.

Common negative results of an inflexible, rigid, out-of-balance lifestyle include: 1) lack of progress because these individuals refuse to try alternatives and do not tolerate the possibility of failure; 2) repeating the same mistakes and experiencing the same poor results, stalemating their thinking processes; 3) easily broken as a result of their inflexibility. Just as an inflexible tree break in a strong wind, these individuals are so rigid and inflexible they break when life delivers unexpected changes or difficulties.

Mitchell was so straight and rigid in his behavior that he lost numerous friends and opportunities. He had been trained in the military to a point of "extra fine tuning"; his particular job in the military would not allow otherwise. Lives depended on Mitch's loyalty and dependability.

While this "square shooter" mentality worked well in the military, after his discharge, Mitch struggled immensely with society and the sloppy ways in which most of the people he encountered lived their lives. His tolerance level for others appeared to be less than zero much of the time, and he reacted the same way toward his own behaviors. He was not at all comfortable with his life but couldn't find the strength or stamina to make the necessary adjustments to meet his expectations.

His employment record demonstrated his impatience with people and his rigid approach to doing things. If his coworkers couldn't do things to satisfy his demands, he simply walked away in anger.

Anyone who has lived with or been around a very rigid individual for any length of time knows how difficult it is to be on guard every moment of the day. Mitch is working on changing, and although finding the change frustrating, he has made a lot of progress. (Suggested strategies: 9, 10, 15, 17, 21, 26)

Flexible
Description:

These individuals have little internal confidence or strength. Their personal and professional progress or success is limited because they lack direction and strong motivation. People struggle with them in social settings and relationships because no one really knows what they think or where they stand. These are "go with the crowd" individuals who lack initiative, personal convictions, and imagination. These individuals are easily swayed because they lack a solid foundation or philosophy on which to hang their thoughts and actions; thus, they are frequently described as followers. They are generally uncomfortable making personal decisions and avoid leadership positions or solitary positions that prohibit feedback from others.

Discussion:

People who are too easily swayed are often perceived as weak, undependable, needy, and directionless. They are easily exploited by others.

At sixteen years old, Joan didn't feel good about herself and felt fortunate when others liked her and wanted her around. She had always been shy and uncomfortable in social settings because she feared others were judging her. In an attempt to feel accepted, she bought friends with food, gifts, and time.

She constantly worried that she wouldn't be able to attract and keep a boyfriend. Because of her anxiety that no one would want her, she was afraid of being alone. This fear prompted her to give in to the desires of her "boyfriends," even though her actions went against her better judgment and values.

She also participated in other activities that were against her principles because she wanted to please others and be liked. Joan was constantly terrified of being abandoned. She eventually ended up in a poor marriage because she was afraid it was her only opportunity for love. She continues to live a life of quiet desperation, wondering what might have been if she had been more discriminating and confident and less easily swayed. (Suggested strategies: 8, 18, 22, 29)

Martha is another example of extreme flexible behavior. Martha was tired of always giving into the requests of others. In therapy, she indicated this had been a problem for as long as she could remember but became especially evident during her adolescent years. She blamed her sexual promiscuity on the fact that she could be talked into almost anything. Even though she had no intention of becoming intimate, she would be worn down by the boy's persistence and constant suggestions of immoral behaviors.

As she discussed her past, she stated she could never remember saying yes but still found herself in sexual situations. She remembers very few details of what led to those inappropriate actions.

This characteristic of being easily swayed carried over into Martha's marriage and parenting roles. Her children and her husband knew they could get what they want from her if they persisted in their requests. Consequently two of the children are struggling in their schoolwork because they persuade their mother they don't have to complete their homework.

Martha and her husband are deeply in debt with no viable means of climbing out of it. Her husband has made costly and shorted-sighted decisions relative to occupations and spending habits. Martha disagreed with most of these decisions, but she could not stand her ground long or strong enough against her husband.

When Martha came in for counseling, she desperately wanted to change her patterns and bring balance to her life. (Suggested strategies: 5, 8, 13, 18, 23, 29)

Individuals like Joan and Martha are too flexible and give up their ability to demonstrate control, one of the essential skills for hula hooping, over their choices. They conclude that they do not have the power to respond as they would like.

Awareness

Where Am I? Where do I want to be?

Directions: Below are descriptions of each barrier extreme. Read them and then decide where you see yourself on the continuum. Circle the number where you think you are. Feel free to ask for help or input from a close friend, spouse, or associate. Remember: Zero signifies balance (our goal). Are you too far to the inflexible side or too far to the flexible side? Where would you rather be?

INFLEXIBLE		FLEXIBLE
Once I have made a decision or a choice, I refuse to move from it. I am not interested in options other than the ones I have selected.	5 4 3 2 1 **0** 1 2 3 4 5	I vacillate from one choice to another, finding it difficult to stick with a choice I have made. I am very affected by what others think and say.

SPONTANEOUS ←→ CAUTIOUS

Spontaneous
Description:

Impulsive or overly spontaneous individuals act now and think later. This is an obvious example of lack of self-control. An old joke—Ready, Fire, Aim—typifies these individuals. In fact, some of these people are so reactive and out of balance, Fire, Ready, Aim might be even more appropriate!

These individuals are generally more reactive rather than proactive. They react to words, behaviors, or situations without thinking. In actuality, they are more controlled by others and external forces than by themselves. In reacting to others, they are at the mercy of those with whom they interact.

People with spontaneous and reactive characters don't think about the long-term possibilities or consequences. They respond to people and situations through emotions. As a result, they rarely give themselves time to generate alternatives reactions, thereby limiting available choices. Extremely spontaneous or impulsive individuals confuse productivity with activity and feel that as long as they are active, they are producing something worthwhile.

Discussion:

Individuals who are impulsive and reactive are fearful of the passing of time and seem to have the philosophy that if they don't take advantage of an opportunity now, it will be forever lost. These individuals have energy and passion and make great followers. A leader is one who considers a multitude of possible choices and makes decisions based on the greatest good. This ability requires conscious, concentrated, and deliberate efforts, character traits that impulsive individuals do not develop or foster. This is a major reason reactive people are rarely productive or effective leaders. They may "lead," but what they accomplish has little lasting value.

An example of someone who is impulsive may be a talented violinist who is in such a hurry to play he does not take time to tune the instrument. As a result, his technique may be flawless and the music precise, but the sound is terrible.

Spontaneous individuals have difficulty understanding that it is generally more profitable and productive to do something methodically than to rush the process. Hence, they don't see the wisdom in the saying, "Haste makes waste." The *continuous motion* principle of hula hooping suggests movement without thought. Similarly, rhythmic cadence and tempo are elements impulsive individuals need to control.

According to Ramona's memory, she was sixteen when she began impulsively spending money when frustrated. She came from a rather well-to-do family, and her parents supplied her with a personal credit card as a means of demonstrating their trust, as well as a strategy of teaching the intricacies of managing money. This approach was a disaster!

Whenever Ramona felt frustrated, which was almost every time she didn't get her own way, she rushed out and bought anything and everything she could find, whether or not she needed it. Her parents tried to convince her of the possible negative consequences of her impulsive behavior, but the lessons didn't remain with her for very long. And her parents bailed her out every time she behaved this way.

In addition to her spending episodes, Ramona also manifested severe temper tantrums and sought isolation. Her nickname, provided by her father, was Pistol, and she certainly lived up to it.

Promiscuity was also part of her reactionary arsenal. Looking back on those years, she says that she didn't care if she even knew the boy; she just wanted to do something that would shock those around her.

CB met Ramona because she had run up more than $30,000 in credit card debt a few years into her marriage. At this point in her life she didn't purchase frivolous items; rather, she justified her spending sprees by buying things for the home or the children. She admitted that at times she would buy just to be buying and would do so on an impulse.

Luckily (maybe), her husband worked in the medical profession and made enough money, with some effort, to bail the family out of financial trouble. But he insisted on Ramona receiving therapy to find a solution to her impulsive behavior.

Ramona conquered her impulsive spending. CB spoke to her several years after therapy, and she mentioned how frightened she had been when she thought she was so far out of balance that she could not be helped and that her marriage was doomed. Her values, her husband's support, her love for their five children, and her own desire to be in balance and control provided enough motivation for her to overcome her earlier problems. In fact, she is extremely (but not to the extreme) stable at this time in her life. (Suggested strategies: 9, 13, 15, 19, 21, 29)

Cautious

Description:

Extremely cautious or distracted individuals are often fearful of making a wrong decision or missing the best opportunity, so they wait and wait for the perfect time or for others to lead the way. Unfortunately, they frequently discover that the opportunity is lost.

People who are out of balance in this direction are like the violin player mentioned previously, only they are so intent on tuning their violin, they never get around to playing it. Many of these individuals confess that they suffer from the "analysis paralysis" syndrome: they recognize that they think too much and that their intentions seldom translate into real, consistent, or meaningful actions.

Discussion:

Many consider these cautious characteristics safer than the impulsive or reactive ones, but indecision can bring its own set of problems. Either extreme represents unbalance and will likely place a strain or burden on close interpersonal relationships. The cautious extreme is problematic because these people do not maintain any predictable, consistent, or productive direction, which in turn creates tension with those with whom they interact.

They also share a common characteristic—procrastination. They become paralyzed by the amount of work they see ahead or are hesitant to move into action because they lack confidence in themselves. Many have witnessed individuals who are unable to make the hula hoop complete two spins around their hips because they are so cautious and fearful of failure they fail to get it started.

Others are able to get the hula hoop spinning but become so fearful of making a mistake they break the rhythm or cadence by altering or discontinuing their physical efforts.

Dr. Jensen is one individual who has not realized his full potential because of his overly cautious behavior. A well-respected and knowledgeable physician, Dr. Jensen is gifted with tremendous abilities as a teacher, clinician, and friend. However, one visible flaw is his problem with slow or late responses and distractibility. He is brilliant, but many are unable to tap into his brilliance because of his scatteredness.

Dr. Jensen can discuss anything in his field of medicine with ease and in a way that even a layperson can understand and use. He is an avid reader, writer, researcher, and lecturer. He is constantly in demand professionally. He is concerned, kind, hardworking, compassionate, and caring, but he fails to reach his potential because of his distractibility. He focuses on one thing for a few minutes and then quickly moves to something else.

His outward appearance also reflects internal disarray, and he is frequently disheveled and unkempt. Many recognize his greatness and are drawn to him because of his many wonderful qualities, yet, almost without exception, he is viewed as the absentminded professor. He has great difficulty maintaining his concentration and focus long enough to finish a given task with completeness and quality, which dulls the reflection of his brilliance and knowledge.

Many of his friends and colleagues have recognized and accepted this obvious limitation, but they are also quick to point out the loss of his full potential. Dr. Jensen himself recognizes his disorganization. To compensate for his problem with remaining on task, he has become overly cautious and relies heavily on others.

On one occasion, he missed a speaking engagement because he simply forgot about it. To avoid repeating this mistake, he now requests his host to remind him repeatedly before an engagement. He continues to avoid assignments unless he can have constant reassurance and reminders.

On one hand, asking for help with this area of personal weakness represents a healthy attitude. However, Dr. Jensen has regressed from an able and confident professional to one with little confidence in his own abilities. (Suggested strategies: 2, 8. 11, 12, 13, 26, 30)

Awareness

Where am I? Where do I want to be?

Directions: Below are descriptions of each barrier extreme. Read them and then decide where you see yourself on the continuum. Circle the number where you think you are. Feel free to ask for help or input from a close friend, spouse, or associate. Remember: Zero signifies balance (our goal). Are you too far to the spontaneous side or too far to the cautious side? Where would you rather be?

SPONTANEOUS		CAUTIOUS
I do things without thinking about any immediate or possible long-range results. Whatever I feel like doing, I do, and I do it now.	54321 **0** 12345	Many times I don't do anything because I don't know what to do or else I am distracted by something else that commands my attention at that time.

CONTROLLING ←→ APATHETIC

Controlling
Description:

Controlling or aggressive individuals have a strong need for control; it feels safer and is more fun. Controllers are generally motivated by the domination of others. They feel they know best and, more often than not, wrongly believe they are serving the greater good. They rarely demonstrate concern for others. They are task oriented rather than people or principle oriented.

Many individuals with this characteristic are covering their insecurity and lack of self-confidence with their outward, superficial, and pretended assertiveness.

Controlling men are tolerated by most, though disliked and considered obnoxious, while aggressive women are avoided and often detested by both genders.

Discussion:

Although controlling individuals can be quite productive, their success often comes at a high cost. They may be able to force or intimidate others into higher productivity in the workplace, and they may always get what they want anywhere else, but they are generally not respected or well thought of. To be too controlling suggests death to any attempt at productive coordination, a necessary skill for both hula hooping and experiencing balance in life.

Harmony between individuals is generally impossible if one or the other is out of balance in their controlling behaviors. Thinking that "might is right" lulls these people into believing that the end justifies the means. Most often those surrounding these individuals do not appreciate the manipulation. It is not uncommon to see such domination of others as a precursor to verbal and physical abuse. This is often evidenced when controllers are confronted by questions or defiance from others.

We must, however, recognize the vast difference between aggressiveness and assertiveness. Individuals who are aggressive attempt to bully, intimidate, threaten, or control others to obtain their perceived rights or a personal goal. These individuals, like porcupines, generally sleep alone. It should not come as a shock that no one enjoys nor seeks to be around them.

Such caustic traits are generally learned from parents or other authority figures rather than inherited. It is something one "does" rather than what one "is" or "becomes." Aggressive characteristics are often demonstrated by actions, voice tones, expressions, and other body language.

Assertive individuals, on the other hand, are those seeking balance and preservation of personal values, beliefs, and boundaries. They seek to establish or maintain what they believe is right and true in a tactful and kind, yet firm and unwavering manner. It is often comforting and reassuring to be in the company of assertive individuals, and the experience is much different than being around aggressive and controlling ones. It is a distinctly unpleasant experience to associate with aggressive and controlling individuals.

David was a thirteen-year-old who was brought into the office by his mother and stepfather. David was becoming increasingly verbally and physically aggressive at home.

David's mother reported that he had always been small for his age. She related that he had been constantly teased and harassed because of his prominent ears, and he took the abuse without retribution. David's parents had met often with school officials in attempts to curb the teasing of their son. However, the teasing behaviors continued unabated.

David's mother finally suggested that he fight back, so during the next week, he hit one of the boys who continually teased him. Although David was suspended from school, the word got around and the kids never teased him again. It appears David developed a newfound skill—control through aggression. He became more verbally aggressive and disrespectful to his sister and mother. In fact, his mother admitted, "We walk around on eggshells in order to avoid upsetting David."

Even his stepfather, who wasn't afraid of David personally, was reluctant to discipline him for fear of being reported for child abuse. David had threatened to call the police after a spanking a few months earlier. Consequently, David's behavior continued to grow in frequency and severity. David's aggression was fostered by his ability to intimidate and control others.

David's temper grew until it was consistently out of control. This had an alarming affect on his family and peers. No one wanted anything to do with him. In fact, his anger and violent behavior led to his hospitalization for one week. Interestingly enough, but not surprising, he was a perfect gentleman while in the hospital. Clearly, he was smart enough to recognize the influence his behavior would have in determining his length of stay.

His family was thrilled with his change and anticipated his return home. However, upon his return, his behavior continued as before.

David's parents brought him into the office. We spent time discussing his aggressive and controlling behavior. We (including David) agreed that everyone was unhappy. However, David felt stuck. In order to be happy, he felt he had to give up power and control, yet he enjoyed the newfound respect, which seemed to lead to unhappiness.

David demonstrated some of his intimidating behavior during therapy. DB was impressed that this small thirteen-year-old could speak to his parents in such a manner without consequences. DB confronted David regarding his behavior, and not only did his behavior stop, but he began to cry. Truly his anger, aggression, and control were inconsistent with his basic values and good nature.

David reluctantly admitted he reveled in his power to control others through his aggression and anger, but he also felt grossly out of control, which was frightening for him. (Suggested strategies: 1, 8, 9, 13, 17, 23, 26, 28, 29)

Apathetic
Description:

Apathetic or passive individuals are also people who seek to control others. However, they do so in a passive or nonaggressive way. For instance, let's say a group of coworkers want to take a fellow colleague out to dinner prior to his departure for another job assignment. Someone asks where he wants to eat, and he replies, "I don't care."

The group persists, saying again, "No, this is your last day with us, and we want to take you to where you want to go." Again, a passive, noncommittal response: "Wherever you guys want to go is fine with me."

Someone may become more directive in order to move the dinner along, asking, "Well, what sounds better, Italian, Mexican, American, or Chinese?"

Again, our passive individual replies, "Anything sounds good."

Notice how he controls through his passivity and apathy. In essence, he evades what the group wants, which is to go to dinner where *he* wants to go. He is controlling others by not giving them what they want, a direct answer. This behavior serves to avoid taking responsibility for one's behavior. Being noncommittal is also a way of maintaining self-preservation and self-protection.

Paradoxically, because these individuals also generally lack specific goals and direction, they seem to wait and depend on others for direction and motivation. Yet when others provide structure and direction, they tend to resent it and view it as controlling. Unfortunately, such passive responses have been previously learned and rewarded.

Discussion:

Sometimes passive or apathetic personality traits indicate the lack of a positive self-concept or self-confidence. Apathetic approaches are often unproductive; at best, their productivity is slow and hindered. Because of their personality, these individuals allow themselves to be used and abused by others and then blame and resent others as well as themselves for what they experience. Their behavior produces and encourages feelings of disdain and distance from family, peers, and colleagues.

Those who are passive and apathetic often want to do things a certain way but instead cater to the wishes of others. This may persist for some time while their resentment builds. Because they have the potential for sudden and unexpected emotional and physical explosions when their limits have been reached, they often explode with long-standing, pent-up emotions.

As with any unbalance, these individuals are at a real disadvantage. Those who are passive or apathetic find their behavior ineffective. While being passive and apathetic may seem safer, it makes it nearly impossible to obtain your wants and needs because no one knows what you want or need! Although it seems contradictory, it is difficult, if not impossible, to please a person with no opinion.

Matthew was one such individual. Soft spoken and gentle in his approach to life, Matthew was, nonetheless, so far out of balance most people felt uncomfortable around him—even his wife, Brenda. She was beside herself, starving for affection and healthy conversation, but Matt didn't respond.

He enjoyed his work and worked hard at it, and when he returned home, he changed his clothes and headed for the garden. It was simply not on his agenda to spend time with Brenda or their children. He enjoyed them if they came outside and worked with him, but even then, he actually had little interaction with them.

During our sessions, Brenda often berated Matt for his lack of attention and indifference toward her and the marriage. He nodded his head in agreement, smiled, and waited for someone to launch into another subject. He understood what Brenda was saying because he could repeat and paraphrase her wishes and desires, but he could not translate that understanding into action. This couple didn't have major fights but experienced silence and isolation for days at a time.

Another challenge was Matt's unwillingness to say no to his brothers. Whatever they requested, he complied with, even to the point that he chose to go hunting with them when Brenda was within a week or so of delivering one of their four children. He could never figure out why she was so angry and upset. All he knew was he couldn't say no to his brothers.

Eventually, Brenda and Matthew divorced. Following the divorce, Brenda found a new relationship and remarried. Matthew stayed at home, tending his garden and feeding his animals. He remains alone, and in a telephone conversation, he indicated that he was extremely lonely and thinks he made huge mistake letting Brenda go. Being too passive can prove costly. (Suggested strategies: 2, 5, 9, 10, 11, 24, 25, 30)

Awareness

Where am I? Where do I want to be?

Directions: Below are descriptions of each barrier extreme. Read them and then decide where you see yourself on the continuum. Circle the number where you think you are. Feel free to ask for help or input from a close friend, spouse, or associate. Remember: Zero signifies balance (our goal). Are you too far to the controlling side or too far to the apathetic side? Where would you rather be?

CONTROLLING		APATHETIC
I want to control my own life, and I resent anyone else attempting to do so. I also want to control others' lives as much as I can. I feel I am right most of the time and expect others to fall in line or get out of my way.	5 4 3 2 1 **0** 1 2 3 4 5	I don't exert much control over my life. I prefer to follow what others decide. I am extremely easygoing and don't like to make many decisions. I go with the flow.

INDEPENDENT ←→ DEPENDENT

Independent

Description:

To be independent and strong-willed in principle can be a wonderful attribute. However, as we have previously discussed, taking anything to an extreme is generally detrimental. Strong-willed individuals often take this characteristic too far. They become independent to the point that they cannot or will not accept any assistance from others, even when they know they need it.

Independent people must do everything by themselves and in their own way. Extremely independent people are proud of their independent nature. They think they don't need anyone, which strains interpersonal relationships. These individuals are strong-minded and generally make poor friends, spouses, or teammates.

Discussion:

Cooperation, coordination, and synergy, which are so important in relationships, are difficult if not impossible to attain when one partner is a strong-willed person. Many partners of independent or strong-willed individuals are forced into the role of dependent or passive associates. No matter what they attempt to do, it is unacceptable to their counterparts.

Independent individuals lose many opportunities that they might enjoy, because they are unwilling to listen and accept alternatives and suggestions from others. Consequently, they deny themselves potentially wonderful experiences and personal growth. Generally, their independence is situational, and at times, they can be both confused and confusing. They don't want interference from others, yet they complain when they feel abandoned or left alone. Total independence is a one-sided proposition, controlled by them, monitored by them, and maintained by them. Try as they might, they cannot seem to grasp why others find them so difficult to deal with.

Steven is a seventy-year-old man who is the epitome of being independent and strong-willed. Steven has a narrow view of the world and doesn't appear to care if anyone, including his wife and family, understands or agrees with him. He does what he wants and thinks only about what applies to him.

DB met with Steven and Virginia after fifty years of marriage. Steven was "sent in" by Virginia, who was hoping to find a medication to help him become more kind and compassionate. Steven readily admitted that the only reason he was present was because Virginia insisted on it. He didn't see any problems. As a result, he admitted he wasn't motivated to change.

Given his attitude, DB observed that we could try different medication, but he was quick to add that he didn't believe they would be beneficial because Steven did not recognize he had a problem and was not motivated to change. As a result, DB didn't prescribe any new medication, and Steven returned home.

Some time later, DB received a letter from Virginia, pleading for help as she enumerating her concerns about Steven. Virginia reported that Steven "could be nice when he wanted to be," such as in church or with "important" people. Most of the time, however, Steven was negative, pessimistic, and angry.

Virginia reported that Steven only wanted to remain in his room listening to classical music without any interruptions or disturbances. As long as everyone left him alone, there were no problems. However, when his grandchildren knocked on his door to visit with him, he scolded them harshly without opening the door and demanded that he be left alone. He appeared to need no one, not even family.

Virginia and the children were social. They loved to be around others and had a wide range of interests. Virginia was tirelessly volunteering, socializing with her friends and family, and developing hobbies of personal interests. She couldn't understand Steven.

Their relationship deteriorated to the point that Steven stayed in his room and only came out for meals. This was the way he wanted it. Virginia, on the other hand, continually attempted to connect with her husband before she eventually gave up. She gave him only what he wanted: food, intimacy, and solitude. Virginia sought to fulfill her needs elsewhere, through activities with family and friends.

Finally, she had had enough. She expected Steven to be different although he had received what he wanted for years. When I asked why she hadn't divorced Steven previously, she said it was for two reasons: she didn't believe in divorce and she couldn't support herself financially.

Interestingly, Steven readily admitted that he was self-centered and negative, yet he felt no motivation to change. To illustrate his independence and selfishness, Virginia reported that Steven did not want to deal with his family during the Christmas holidays. In spite of his wishes, Virginia scheduled a family party. Steven refused to participate and, in fact, stayed in a hotel over the forty-eight hours of Christmas Eve and Christmas Day. He returned home the day after Christmas. Upon his return, he couldn't understand why Virginia was upset with him. He had only done what he thought was right for him, something he had done throughout their marriage.

In therapy, DB emphasized that both parties were to blame. Steven was extremely independent and strong-willed to the point that he thought of no one but himself. He was kind and courteous only when it served his purposes. Virginia, on the other hand, gave Steven everything he wanted. He received his food, intimacy, and solitude without providing anything in return. This pattern had been established many years ago and had not changed throughout their marriage.

As far as we know, they are still together, each living a life separate and independent of the other. Steven remains oblivious to the enjoyment he could be receiving if he would allow others into his life. (Suggested strategies: 2, 3, 5, 9, 10, 14, 19, 20, 26, 30)

Dependent

Description:

Dependent individuals genuinely lack personal self-confidence and self-esteem. They feel that their thoughts and actions are inferior to others. They often appear needy, requiring help and support in all decisions they make.

As a part of their insecurity, dependent people do not enjoy being alone. They crave the presence and reinforcement of others because of their insecurity about decisions. They are constantly in fear of making the wrong decision.

Those with dependent natures generally seek others to initiate or confirm their thoughts and judgments. These individuals need others for verification and constantly live in fear. However, with the help of others, this fear is lessened. They need others to make it through life.

Discussion:

Individuals who are extremely needy generally developed this pattern as children, when their needy behaviors were reinforced. Once such a pattern has been established, it can be difficult to change. Some people are so needy and dependent that others end up "carrying" them. As a result, a codependent role is often developed where one person depends solely on another and the other is forced into a role of caretaking, whether or not he chooses that role. The caregiver feels obligated to care for the needy individual.

The usual driving force behind such needy behavior is to encourage others to feel and be responsible for the individual. Often, caregivers feel suffocated or smothered by those who are so heavily involved in their lives. Being needed to this extent becomes confining and often produces resentment, which can prove deadly to relationships.

Needy individuals have a way of gaining attention and demanding control of others by their dependence. They get their needs fulfilled without having to return the effort. Friends and family members feel inadequate around needy individuals because, no matter how much is given, it is never enough. Needy people always want and need more. As a result, needy and dependent individuals become cripples in many personal arenas. In their minds, they cannot survive without others. What a difficult and terrifying place to be.

We are social creatures and require interdependence with others. However, there is a significant difference between *needing* a relationship and *desiring* one. Needing a relationship is unhealthy because it requires dependence on another. Dependent people are parasitic in nature and act as if they are unable to function without their "host."

On the other hand, desiring a relationship implies that we are sufficiently independent; we don't *need* someone in order to function. We just enjoy people.

Individuals in healthy relationships recognize and enjoy the balance and benefits obtained by personal space, cooperation, and interdependence.

Janet is a forty-five-year-old woman who has always tried to please her parents and siblings. But no matter what she does, it is never enough. About ten years ago, Janet's mother suffered a debilitating illness. Since that day, family members have rallied around their mother. Many of the children sat with their mother for an entire day, providing the necessary care that comes with such an illness. They washed and bathed her. They shopped for, cared for, and fed her.

Recently, Janet developed chronic fatigue syndrome. She has struggled with the demands of her own poor health, the needs of her own family, and the continued care of her mother. She developed several secondary infections, which inhibited her normal activity levels.

In an attempt at self-preservation, Janet discussed the situation with her family. She was devastated when they were not only unsympathetic toward her but informed her they needed her to care for their mother an additional day because one of her siblings had personal difficulties.

Janet attempted to explain to the family her inability to carry her own load much less take on any additional load, but the family's response to Janet's dilemma was anger and dissatisfaction. Her family members insisted that they couldn't function without her, and an unhealthy environment was established, a situation in which no one will come out ahead.

Our challenge was to assist Janet in establishing and maintaining her personal needs and boundaries without accepting and internalizing the guilt the family produced. (Suggested strategies: 4, 7, 10, 11, 17, 19, 22, 27, 30)

Awareness

Where am I? Where do I want to be?

Directions: Below are descriptions of each barrier extreme. Read them and then decide where you see yourself on the continuum. Circle the number of where you think you are. Don't be afraid to obtain help from a close friend, spouse, or associate.

Remember: Zero signifies balance (our goal). Are you too far on the independent side or too far on the dependent side? Where would you rather be?

INDEPENDENT		DEPENDENT
I get along very well by myself and generally have little need for others. If they don't want to go with me, I will go alone.	54321 **0** 12345	I mainly rely on others and what they want to do. I need them around me to make my decisions and comfort me. I need others to validate my decisions and feelings.

PASSIONATE ←——→ INDIFFERENT

Passionate
Description:

Clearly, many types of passions exist. As we discuss passion in greater detail, we recognize the many extremes possible in this area. We will specifically use anger to illustrate the unbalance that can result from extremes in the area of passion.

Passionate individuals are those who run by emotion. Whenever they are faced with their triggers, logic and rational thought disappear, much like the response of a bull when he sees the color red. There doesn't appear to be any rational reason for this phenomenon—the bull's desire to charge appears to be instinctive.

As a result of their passionate natures, these individuals are at the mercy of incidental situations and the random responses of others. They can function fine until they collide with an unexpected trigger. When this happens, they lose balance and are controlled by their emotions.

A common reason for failing to keep a hula hoop twirling is the loss of concentration because we are distracted by one thing or another. When an overly passionate person allows herself to lose awareness because an emotional trigger has been encountered, cadence is interrupted and motion likely stopped. The result? A hoop falling to the ground. To maintain good balance, we must stay focused and aware of our circumstances and actions.

Discussion:

Anger and the inability to control a temper is evidence that an individual is emotionally out of control. Uncontrolled anger always produces negative consequences, including abuse. Those at whom the anger is directed experience fear and emotional and physical distance. No good can come of uncontrolled anger. (Rash anger should not be confused with "righteous indignation"; which with proper application can play a positive and significant role in life.)

Unfortunately, society often tolerates, accepts, and even encourages anger. An angry outburst is frequently depicted as an appropriate way for people, especially men, to express themselves.

Some individuals view anger or the loss of emotional control as simply a minor weakness. "Boys will be boys," they might say. Or, "he had it coming."

Some people attend sporting events hoping to see a fight break out, if not between the competitors then maybe between the spectators.

Have you ever wondered why people are so enthralled with professional wrestling, boxing, and similar sports? Many crave the excitement of combat that comes when two competitors seek to beat each other into submission. Who hasn't witnessed fans overjoyed at a sports event when two or more athletes lose control in an all-out battle? Although many of us consider the Romans barbaric because of their passion and interest in gladiators fighting to the death, we should ask ourselves, are we much different today?

Anger is generally a secondary emotion, resulting from discouragement, frustration, or confusion. Anger is almost always the result of an individual not getting his way. Learning to deal with the antecedent condition—the discouragement, the frustration, the confusion—is generally much more effective than trying to quell the anger. Power over self and situations can demonstrate true personal strength.

Mitchell and Sandi were a middle-aged couple with four adolescent children. Both had been raised in a small town in Southern Arizona, and they were used to working with farm animals.

Mitch and Sandi wanted to learn how to resolve their differences. In their words, they had a battle royal every time they disagreed. They both attended church regularly and professed to being moderately religious. They were a nice couple, and CB had a difficult time believing their descriptions of the fights they would have.

However, as they arrived for one session, they handed CB a videotape of one of their arguments. Why they would record such a scene is anybody's guess, but they did. CB discovered that they had been telling the truth. These two self-labeled religious individuals became so angry that they verbally tore each another to shreds. The words that came out of their mouths would never have been used in church or in public! It was terrifying to witness how their anger took hold of them. Their fight consisted of yelling, screaming, swearing, pushing, slamming, and throwing, although both insisted they never intended to hit their partner.

Obviously, nothing was resolved, and they eventually retreated to separate rooms and didn't speak until the next day. Apparently, their anger had gotten so out of control in some situations that police officers had been called! Uncontrolled anger is horrific, and Sandi and Mitch were unable to make the necessary changes. Unfortunately, they eventually divorced. (Suggested strategies: 1, 5, 8, 9, 12, 13, 14, 18, 21, 22, 24, 29, 30)

Indifferent
Description:

Individuals who are indifferent appear to maneuver through life without a rudder. People driven by indifference have little if any joy or happiness in life. They generally have no direction, goals, or purpose. They drift, taking their subsistence from whatever comes. They appear to be without any emotion or passion. As a result, they are generally alone because others cannot connect with them.

Discussion:

Passionless or indifferent people are to be pitied. Nothing appears to provide zest or vitality to their lives. They do not seem to enjoy anything and are living a blasé and unmotivated life. In addition, they seem emotionless, which makes them even more difficult to connect with. These individuals are difficult to read and to develop deep feelings toward.

As others attempt to interact with them, they block any engagement, connection, or negotiation. They often send the message that others' associations and opinions do not matter or even exist. It is difficult to communicate with or gather information from indifferent people because no one can read their true emotional state. Therefore, no point of reference is provided to assess direction, condition, or attitude.

Emotionally flat individuals are often manipulated by stronger personalities. Their silence and indifference generally increase their distance from others, which often results in isolation.

Perry is one such individual. Employed as a junior high school teacher, Perry generally taught the office machine classes, specializing in computers. He was laid back and easy to get along with. His students loved him because of his gentle nature; he never seemed riled, regardless of what went on in his classroom.

When Perry came home each afternoon, his behavior was very predictable. He arrived home somewhat fatigued, so he took a short nap. After his nap, he retired to his computer room and either read a magazine or played on the computer. Family members seldom saw him other than at mealtime, and sometimes not even then because he took his plate into "his retreat."

When Perry and his wife, Mary, came in for therapy, their marriage was at a low ebb. Mary was starving for attention and affection, neither of which Perry felt capable of or willing to provide. He did not manifest any passion in life, except for those activities that provided him isolation from others. Even in therapy, he never changed expressions. It seemed as if he merely existed.

Changes in his attitudes and actions did not occur, and the marriage ended in divorce. Where did Perry settle? He could be found in a small apartment with just enough room for his computer and his magazines. (Suggested strategies: 2, 5, 8, 9, 11, 12, 13, 14, 20, 26)

Extreme indifference spells death to most endeavors, including hula hooping. Without enough interest in something, people make no attempt at coordination. Any cadence is irregular because of lack of interest, and an individual may not care enough about what is going on to move at all.

Awareness

Where am I? Where do I want to be?

Directions: Below are descriptions of each barrier extreme. Read them and then decide where you see yourself on the continuum. Circle the number where you think you are. Feel free to ask for help or input from a close friend, spouse, or associate. Remember: Zero signifies balance (our goal). Are you too far to the passionate side or too far to the indifferent side? Where would you rather be?

PASSIONATE		INDIFFERENT
I have a short fuse and those around me know it. I sometimes have trouble controlling my anger, and in those situations, I will likely lose my temper. It is the only way people will listen to me. I find it provides me with attention and control.	54321**0**12345	I don't react much to what goes on around me, mainly because I don't really care. I just seem to go through life, generally being neither happy nor sad. I am a "whatever" individual.

FEARFUL ⟷ FEARLESS

Fearful
Description:

Many individuals suffer from fearfulness and insecurity, destructive and paralyzing feelings that block active and productive thoughts and actions. Fearful individuals are plagued by the hypothetical question: "What if?" They are uneasy in large groups and around people they don't know. They are afraid to make new friends. They are terrified of leaving their comfort zones. They are afraid of going out and learning and doing new things.

Discussion:

It is helpful for us to differentiate between rational and irrational fears. Rational fears are those grounded in reality and understood by anyone in the same position. For example, let's say someone earns $2,000 per month but is spending $4,000 per month. Almost everyone would find this situation fearful, problematic, and troubling.

An irrational fear, on the other hand, may be someone who is the captain of the football team and a class officer and is dating several popular girls—yet still continually worries that he is not liked or accepted by others. This clearly is a fear most individuals would consider irrational and find difficult to understand.

Unfortunately, either type of fear, rational or irrational, can hinder progression and potential.

Fear is a common result of ignorance or faulty (inaccurate, incomplete, or unclear) information. When we surround ourselves with individuals who view the world with pessimism, their fear and insecurity can be contagious. We have worked with children who have witnessed fearful and insecure parents, friends, and associates, who have modeled and infected others with this spirit of fear and insecurity. Our attitudes and actions relative to fear can and do *affect* and *infect* others!

Ann had grown up in such a home. A well-intentioned mother constantly bombarded Ann about her decisions and the various dangers fraught in society. Ann indicated that whatever she chose to do, no matter how minor, her mother voiced fear and concern about the decision. Ann reported that on one occasion she told her mother that she was going to the local mall to shop. However, when Ann's mother became aware of the route Ann was taking, she asked her why she would take such a dangerous route.

Ann soon developed a general fear and insecurity about anything outside of her own home. She reached the point where she would not venture away from her home without her husband. She constantly called him at work for reassurance and help throughout the day. Eventually, she came in for therapy, recognizing that she was incapacitated by her fears and anxiety.

Though the process was slow, Ann slowly became willing and able to risk and eventually developed the courage to try new things. She confronted something she had always feared—the water—by taking swimming lessons and learning to swim. She also traveled away from home without her husband or friends. Ann was extremely grateful to put her paralyzing fears and insecurities completely behind her. (Suggested strategies: 1, 7, 12, 13, 18, 23, 26, 28, 30)

In Ann, we saw how the attitudes and actions of someone else, in her case, her mother, infected and afflicted others. In Ann's case, her mother's actions produced a great dependency on others. If she had been unable to build enough confidence to take risks, Ann would have been unable to develop her true potential.

Fear and faith cannot exist in the same place at the same time. This is similar to the relationship between darkness and light, where one cannot exist in the presence of the other. Fear and insecurity can be brought into submission, although it may take concerted work and effort to reach a healthy balance. However, it is worth it!

Fearless

Description:

Fearless, reckless individuals are accidents waiting to happen. They are generally impulsive, minimally conscious of consequences, and often described as "adrenalin junkies." They live for the moment, thriving on activities that are likely to produce harm and accident. Unfortunately, they often risk the lives of others along with their own in their enthusiasm and drive for pleasure and enjoyment.

Reckless people can be typified by the phrase: "I feel the need for speed!" Regrettably they possess the dangerous combinations of impulsivity, carelessness, and fearlessness. Because of their reckless determination, they often arrive at consequences for which they are unprepared. The dye has been cast, and in an instant, lives can be changed forever.

Such fearless and reckless individuals are generally selfish, failing to consider the possible consequences of their behavior on others. Although this group is self-absorbed, they are not content to do activities alone and want others to enjoy what they seek. As a result, the pressure and control they exert on others creates a definite unbalance and can produce distance in their relationship with others. Unfortunately, those who are not as strong give in to this pressure and experience many of the same results.

Discussion:

At first, we may admire someone who is fearless. As we watch various actors walk on the wings of airplanes or wrestle wild animals, we wonder at their ability to perform such feats of danger. Anyone can be impressed as someone dives on top of an eight-foot crocodile and wrestles it into submission.

However, as with things of this world, the excitement and fun eventually wears off. Larry personifies this particular extreme. He had chosen fire fighting as his profession and constantly sought adventures that would literally place his life in jeopardy. His adventures included skydiving, scuba diving, mountain climbing, and auto racing. He volunteered for any and all experiences he thought would provide the "rush" he constantly sought.

After two serious accidents and a surgery, Larry settled down enough to get married and start a family. But the change was not permanent, and within two years, he was yearning for excitement. This caused Betsy, his wife, great concern. She had tried, prior to the birth of their son, to join Larry in some of his exotic experiences but now found these endeavors too unsafe and uncomfortable.

Apparently her fears carried little weight when pitted against the reckless nature of her husband, and Larry refused to alter his regained lifestyle. To make his life even more exciting, he began spending time with women who also lived on the wild side. Before too long, he was unfaithful to his wife. Betsy was devastated and threatened to leave him. However, his deep love for his son persuaded Larry to attempt another change of lifestyle. But to no avail. The change lasted less than two months, and he proved unfaithful again. This was the nail in the marriage coffin, and although neither had desired a divorce, the unbalance in Larry's life proved too great for marital stability. He had chosen to continue his extreme and reckless behavior, and it had cost him his marriage and family. As with most extremes, everyone lost. (Suggested strategies: 2, 4, 8, 9, 11, 21, 30)

Awareness

Where am I? Where do I want to be?

Directions: Below are descriptions of each barrier extreme. Read them and then decide where you see yourself on the continuum. Circle the number where you think you are. Feel free to ask for help or input from a close friend, spouse, or associate. Remember: Zero signifies balance (our goal). Are you too far to the fearful side or too far to the fearless side? Where would you rather be?

FEARFUL		FEARLESS
I am very uneasy being around people I don't know and doing things I haven't done before. There are times when my fears block me from going places and doing things I would like to do. It is safer for me.	5 4 3 2 1 **0** 1 2 3 4 5	I will try almost anything once. I love to take risks and gambles in life. I am also not interested in what impact my reckless behavior might have on those around me.

PESSIMISTIC ←——→ OPTIMISTIC

Pessimistic
Description:

Extremely pessimistic individuals are negative. They generally sit alone. They are not fun to be around because they tend have little hope for the future or a positive vision of themselves or others. As a result of this pessimism, they commonly lack the disposition or motivation to change their uncomfortable circumstances. Often these individuals revel in "pity parties."

Although their general goal is to obtain sympathy and attention from others, they will likely discount any positive contact or comment made. Because of their unbalance in personal responsibility, they excuse their lack of success on external elements. They tend to blame others for their inability to reach their fullest potential. These individuals desire evidence, reassurance, and confirmation from others in support of their negativity, and they pay little attention to anything that would counteract their discouraging attitude.

Discussion:

Pessimistic individuals seldom, if ever, radiate happiness, satisfaction, or contentment because they don't feel these sensations. They appear to be searching for something more. They see the bad side of each and every situation, which makes it difficult for others to communicate with them in any healthy or positive way. Pessimistic people have the ability to squeeze all the fun out of life. Their remarkable ability to find the negative, in even the most neutral settings, acts like porcupine quills maintaining distance and isolation. Due to their shortsightedness and negativity, others are uncomfortable around them and find it depressing to be in their presence.

Vince's parents did the best they could to rear and train their eight children under extremely trying circumstances, including the Great Depression. Although his parents stayed together for more than sixty years, Vince was not sure they were ever really happy. Vince's mother found enjoyment through relationships with her siblings. His father, on the other hand, was not much of a social person and found consolation in the bottle. Of course, that only made matters worse for him and the family.

As Vince looked back, he could not decide which came first, the negativism or the drinking, but they certainly made comfortable bedfellows and seemed to feed off each other. Over the years Vince's father appeared incapable of seeing the world as a good, positive, enjoyable place. In his mind, nothing worked out for him or the family, and everyone he met had a personal agenda that prevented any trust. He had little faith or confidence in anyone or any institution. To him, everyone was on the take, and in fact, many people did take advantage of him.

Vince's dad meant well, but nothing was ever good enough. He constantly found fault with everyone and everything. Looking back, Vince realized this as one of the most difficult issues they faced as children. They could never please their dad or make him proud—at least he never mentioned it to them if he was. He lacked balance in his perspective of life and seldom smiled as a result. Now in his late nineties, he just sits and thinks about the past. It appears as if only negative memories remain.

Vince regrets that his father suffered because of his negativism. His last few years were spent in an old rocking chair, doing nothing. He even forgot to eat.

In Vince's father's case, there certainly wasn't any motion, let alone continuous motion! Clearly, more balanced thoughts and behaviors might have brought some peace and joy in the last years of this man's life. (Suggested strategies: 5, 8, 10, 14, 20, 23, 28, 30)

Optimistic
Description:

Extremely optimistic individuals don't just view the world through rose-colored glasses, they live in a rose-colored world where only happiness exists. This attitude places them at great risk of being manipulated by others. People who refuse to face reality tend to be insensitive to the serious feelings or situations of others. Their interpersonal relationships suffer because it is difficult to relate or get close to them because of their "pie in the sky" mentality.

Overly optimistic individuals reduce everything to its most simplistic and basic source, and they do not recognize the complications or nuances of people's lives. They may not allow others to feel the natural pain and discouragement that comes with many common experiences of life.

Discussion:

Because optimistic people often possess unrealistic and simplistic views of the world, their fantasies create unreasonable expectations of others. They frequently miss or ignore problems that, if handled while small, could more easily be addressed. However, because of their exaggerated optimism and denial, overly optimistic individuals allow these situations to grow until something that was small and easily fixed becomes serious and more difficult to resolve.

A common hallmark of overly optimistic individuals is their tendency to dream more than to do. They have tremendous ideas that are seldom brought to fruition, and they often wonder why things don't turn out as they had envisioned. They don't understand why their lives remain stagnant and their dreams fail to materialize. Their unbalance in this area causes them to see "beyond the mark."

We used to think that being optimistic was a wonderful trait for anyone to have—until we met Richard. Richard was so optimistic it was almost unbearable to be around him. His constant smiles, which his teenage daughter called a cheesy grin, were not engaging but puzzling and disconcerting. He was so positive about life that he failed to connect with reality much of the time.

The larger problem was that, not only did Richard have his own problems facing reality, he expected, or rather demanded, everyone in his house view life the same way. His marriage and family relationships were in shambles according to all family members, but to him everything was just wonderful. He was so far out of balance in this area that neither his wife nor his children felt they were allowed to have problems. How could they, in Richard's perfectly marvelous world?

The fact was, Richard's wife and children were miserable living with him. After several verbal and physical battles between parents and children, Richard saw the need for serious help; however, he felt it was the other family members who needed the help rather than him! He thought that if someone from the outside would tell them how wonderful their lives were, they would be happy.

In this case, that didn't happen because CB did not buy into his fantasy. Things went from bad to worse until one of the family members ended up spending the night in jail after Richard called the police over a seemingly small matter. Even that experience did not wipe the smile off Richard's face. CB ran into him sometime later, and he was still smiling. When CB asked him how his family was doing, he replied, as he always had, "Everything is wonderful!" CB knew better. (Suggested strategies: 3, 10, 14, 24, 30)

Awareness

Where am I? Where do I want to be?

Directions: Below are descriptions of each barrier extreme. Read them and then decide where you see yourself on the continuum. Circle the number where you think you are. Feel free to seek feedback from a spouse or close friends and associates. Remember: Zero signifies balance (our goal). Are you too far on the pessimistic side or too far on the optimistic side? Where would you rather be?

PESSIMISTIC		OPTIMISTIC
Things never work out the way I think they should or the way I would like them to. I see only the problems in life, the dark side. I have little hope for the future.	5 4 3 2 1 **0** 1 2 3 4 5	I view the world through a rose-colored glass. Although unrealistic, I only want to see the bright, happy side of things. My world is not real.

INFERIORITY ⬌ SUPERIORITY

Inferiority
Description:

Individuals with a low sense of self-worth are unforgiving of their own frailties and weaknesses. As a result, they are extremely hard on themselves, harder than anyone else would be. Their vision is so overshadowed by their faults, they are unable to view the world in a complete or objective way. They are often full of doubt and fear regarding their own value and generally perceive themselves as inferior to others; therefore, they feel they have little to offer.

These individuals have a difficult time accepting genuine compliments from others. "If you really knew me like I know me," they think, "you wouldn't like me. You would be horrified and disappointed." In the extreme, they may see themselves so low and without redeeming qualities that they are unworthy of being loved. Individuals who see themselves as inferior have negative thoughts and attitudes, which continue to worsen. Their thinking follows this pattern of thinking: Self-Doubt → Fear → Inactivity → Failure → Low Self-Esteem → Increased Self-doubt. If ever a formula explained why frequent failure with the hula hoop occurs, this would be it.

Discussion:

We know ourselves best, including our weaknesses and imperfections. These flaws may be magnified as we interact with others and compare ourselves to them. This negative self-view develops into negative thoughts and actions, as well as self-doubts.

Sources of self-doubt or inferiority include criticism from others, previous failures, lack of experience, lack of training or ability, unrealistic expectations, and unrealistic comparisons with others. The devil loves to use the tools of self-doubt and inferiority. If he can paralyze, detain, and retard us, his evil purposes will succeed.

Many individuals have inferiority feelings as the result of comparing themselves with others. We must remember that all comparisons are unfair and inaccurate because no two people or circumstances are alike. No one in the universe is like us. No man can read our true thoughts and feelings or the intent of our hearts. This is one of the reasons we have been instructed to withhold judgment of others. We can't know all the facts about people's lives.

We could learn something from every person we meet. Everyone we meet is better at something than we are. Some are able to paint or draw with accuracy and emotion, and some may play a musical instrument with ease and beauty. Some may be gifted with computers or mechanical abilities while others are able to work with and enjoy people.

When we can appreciate the talents of others, we are inspired and uplifted, but when we compare ourselves to them the result is usually destructive and discouraging. Typically our worst critic is ourself. Many of us are kind and forgiving to others, yet cruel, mean, impatient, and degrading to our own souls.

One concept we have tried to teach our patients is that what we believe about ourselves today is the result of the continuous feedback we have received from the world around us since the time of our birth. When we came into this world we were clean, pure, and innocent. However, as we grew older, things changed. Because those around us loved us and wanted to help us, they sometimes bombarded us with criticism and correction to make us better. Parents and teachers often paid more attention to what we did wrong than what we did correctly.

For instance, if we brought home a report card with four "A's" and one "C," our parents typically focused on the "C." Their intentions were to help us, but hearing too many corrections over too long a time convinced us that we were not as good as we once thought and that, no matter how well we did, we could never meet their expectations.

At this point, the positive picture we had of ourselves became overshadowed by a negative view that discouraged us and weakened our self-confidence. Wanting to be well thought of and well received by others, we thought we needed to develop at least the appearance of a positive self-concept. Even though we knew our positive appearance was not genuine, it served as a defense and protection from the unkind, harsh criticisms and judgment of others. We couldn't let others see what was actually inside of us because our true and good self had been hidden by the negative image we had developed.

In order to achieve balance, we need to uncover, foster, and expand the true self that resides within us. Doing so will help us attain the balance we seek.

Let's review several definitions so we can more clearly understand our true nature and value.

Self-Concept (how I think about myself): Our self-concept is related to any information we receive from external data and then integrate into our view of ourselves.

Self-Image (how I see myself reflected back from others): Our self-image is how we perceive ourselves as we relate to others and they relate to us. We receive perceptions and data from others about our different roles as a spouse, parent, employee, church worker, friend, or neighbor. Developing this image requires a reflector of some kind, similar to a mirror.

Self-Confidence (how I do things): Our self-confidence is related to our abilities and skills in different areas of our lives. For example, we may have high confidence in our ability to play the piano but low confidence in our ability to fix the engine in our car. Our self-confidence can wax or wane depending on our experiences.

Self-Esteem (how I feel about the above attributes): Our self-esteem is a composite of the areas mentioned above.

Self-Worth (my basic worth): Interestingly, we believe our self-worth has nothing to do with skills, talents, or abilities. In fact, it has nothing to do with the four elements noted above. *We have true worth simply because we live and breathe!*

Jeff is a thirty-year-old, hardworking, honest, generous, and capable business owner. In high school, he was known as a partier, and he generally preferred to do anything but study. Jeff is well liked and has always been surrounded by family, friends, and associates. He has what many would call a restless spirit and has participated in innumerable activities; his special loves include family and couple vacations, snowmobiling, and associating with friends. He adores the outdoors and is great fun to be around.

Jeff is extremely bright and has special talents for mechanical and hands-on activities. A natural leader, Jeff is well respected and seems to be successful in any endeavor he attempts. He also has many interests in community and philanthropic undertakings.

Jeff and his lovely wife, Marion, married shortly after high school, and they have two children. Early in their married life, Jeff and Marion began a small business. Through hard work, ingenuity, and sound business practices, the business flourished. As the business grew, they hired additional employees, and their business is now a prominent part of their community and provides a significant number of jobs and revenue.

Although Jeff has a wonderful family and is well known, respected, and wealthy, he views his life as a failure. He has three reasons for his misperception: 1) He did not do well academically and did not obtain a college education. 2) He is a perfectionist and is never satisfied with where he is or what he does. 3) Jeff has an inferior view of himself.

To any outsider, Jeff is clearly successful. Yet, he robs himself of happiness because he feels inferior and lacks a sense of self-worth. Tragically, his feelings of inferiority are self-induced; he is his own worst enemy.

Jeff doesn't want to feel this way any more. He recognizes that he is successful in what is most important, yet that knowledge hasn't translated into his everyday thoughts and actions. However, he is motivated to change and is making slow but steady progress. (Suggested strategies: 4, 6, 10, 13, 14, 21, 23)

Superiority

Description:

These individuals see themselves as superior to and better than everyone else. They have little or no patience with others. They often brag about their abilities and speak condescendingly to others and about others. Because these individuals need to feel superior, they make comparisons and judgments of others, which harms their relationships with others.

Discussion:

Some suggested that if your feelings of superiority are based in fact, then feeling superior is acceptable. However, if we are honest with ourselves, we recognize that no one feels comfortable around those who feel and act superior. When you think about people you respect and enjoy being around, this characteristic is never found.

Viewing ourselves as superior damages both us and those around us. This attitude drives a wedge between individuals. Everyone wants to be accepted, respected, and liked for who they are, and that doesn't happen when you're dealing with people who feel superior.

Another aspect of this is when people develop a particular skill or high level of competence and then talk about how simple or easy it is to do. The skill may be repairing cars, playing the piano, teaching lessons, giving talks, or even keeping a hula hoop spinning. Keep in mind that balanced individuals have no need to brag abut their skills and abilities.

Sometimes individuals who consider themselves superior in intellect also feel they are superior physically. A very slender man, Brent was an avid walker, runner, and biker. He looked great and was extremely healthy. His wife, Betty, on the other hand, did not share his athletic ability or his determination to eat healthy. She was approximately thirty pounds overweight, and although she wanted to lose the weight, she was having a difficult time. Brent didn't help at all! He constantly criticized her and was often rude. In Brent's opinion, anyone could be skinny if they wanted to. If he could be in such great shape, so could she!

With patience wearing thin on both ends, this marriage was heading for divorce, something each partner had experienced in earlier marriages. His intolerance, superior attitude, condescension, and rudeness were taking their toll on Betty's spirit and willingness to remain in the marriage, and he wouldn't back off. He wanted a wife as skinny as he was, and he would not settle for anything less. Again and again, he held himself up as the perfect example for her to follow.

Obviously Brent was out of balance and out of line. The problem with this relationship was not so much Betty's weight as it was his attitude of superiority.

Betty finally reached her limit and told Brent that she was through and she hoped he could find a skinny wife to take care of him for the rest of his life. She had had it! Initially, Brent shrugged off the threat and puffed out his chest as he waltzed out of the room.

Fortunately, this story has a happy ending. Brent left that night and spent time alone, thinking about what he was about to lose. He talked to a close friend, who told him that same thing he had heard in counseling.

Finally humble, Brent realized the scope and danger of his superior attitude and vowed to change.

And change he did. He returned to Betty, apologized for his mistreatment of her, and promised to love and accept her, regardless of her weight. He would never bring the subject up again, he said, and would help her if she asked him. His apologies were genuine, and Betty was touched. They reconciled.

Brent remains slender, and Betty has maintained her weight; she may even have lost a pound or two. They ride bikes together at her pace and are now meeting one another on an equal level, both in balance with where they are. (Suggested strategies for Brent: 3, 5, 10, 14, 21, 24, 30)

Awareness

Where am I? Where do I want to be?

Directions: Below are descriptions of each barrier extreme. Read them and then circle the number where you think you are. Feel free to ask for feedback from a spouse or close friends and associates. Remember: Zero signifies balance (our goal). Are you too far on the inferiority side or too far on the superiority side? Where would you rather be?

INFERIORITY		SUPERIORITY
I cannot compete with others in life. I am of less worth because of what I am unable to contribute. I do not feel good about myself.	5 4 3 2 1 **0** 1 2 3 4 5	I tend to see most people as beneath me, and I have little patience with their incompetence. I feel I can do about anything I set my mind to.

DIRECTIONLESS ◄─► CONGESTED

Directionless
Description:

People who suffer from boredom or the lack of direction admit to being unhappy, yet they lack the motivation to change their situations. They look to friends and family to be entertained. They don't set goals, and they lack ambition. They often spend a lot of time doing mindless things or nothing at all. Their lack of mental stimulation produces dull thinking.

Discussion:

Without direction and goals, we are like a ship adrift on the ocean and left to the mercy of the winds and currents to carry us wherever they will. Without direction, we can't measure our progress. In fact, there isn't likely to be any progress to measure. We all must be stimulated and stretched to reach our greatest potential.

Jonathan fits this description. He is seventeen years old and came to the office accompanied by his mother, who expressed grave concern about her son. She indicated he was continually unhappy, and she thought it was because he was bored and had no purpose or direction.

Jon wasn't really interested in counseling. As we spoke, he offered one-word answers to questions. He admitted he did not have any goals and was doing poorly in all areas of his life. He did not enjoy his church, had difficulty in peer relationships, and performed poorly in school, although he was a very bright young man. Jon avoided family functions, schoolwork, and church activities.

Jon's only interest was skateboarding with his friends. Jon's mother described his friends as very "dark" personalities. In her eyes, they were also depressive, directionless, and negative in nature. Jon's parents worried about his poor choices and the lack of the direction in his life, yet they were limited in how they could help him change.

Every time I saw Jon, he was in a depressed, dark, and angry mood; he was clearly out of balance and unhappy. Although Jon did make some changes, his motivation was to "get my parents off my back" so he could skateboard. Unfortunately, that motivation wasn't sufficient enough for lasting change. (Suggested strategies: none are applicable until Jon indicates at least some motivation for change.)

Congested
Description:

Individuals who struggle with overcommitment or being too busy experience significant stress when they realize they have overextended themselves yet again. They are often frustrated by demands that keep coming at them from so many different directions. Most overcommitted individuals recognize that when they are torn in so many directions they can't and don't do their best work. The usual result of this condition is the lack of satisfaction that comes from a job well done.

These individuals are always tired and continually wish for more energy. They certainly demonstrate the hula-hooping skill of continuous motion, but this motions is so scattered and unfocused it does not keep the hoop around the hooper's waist. Other hooping skills are also affected. Coordination is next to impossible because of the busy schedule. Concentration becomes a barrier to the chosen life style, and control is given to the situation rather than the individual.

Discussion:

We frequently see individuals who struggle with this issue. They struggle to prioritize the numerous demands on their time and eliminate the elements of lesser value. Most of us are familiar with this challenge; most of us have occasionally lost focus of our most important and significant priorities. However, unbalanced people over-commit time after time.

People over-commit for many reasons. Over-commitment is often due to personal pride. Sometimes we not only feel that we *can* do everything but that we *should* do everything. Often we do too many things because we are seeking the praise of others. And some of us over-commit in an attempt to prove our worth to ourselves and to others.

Frequently choosing to be overcommitted or too busy results from the inability or unwillingness to say no. Overcommitted people want to—and feel like they should—help everyone. However, we need to remember that we all have limited time, energy, abilities, and resources, and we simply cannot be all things to all people. It is impossible, and trying puts us out of balance and produces suffering.

Setting goals and establishing priorities can help produce the results we all desire. Saying no to one thing is nothing more than saying yes to a higher priority. Practicing this skill makes us wiser, more productive individuals.

We like this entertaining analogy, which illustrates how we can be our own worst enemy. A boa constrictor was slithering through the jungle, just as he did every day. As you know, a boa is a snake that consumes its prey whole. On this day, the boa was slithering along the jungle floor and ran across a young rabbit. Without hesitation, he pounced on the rabbit, quickly consuming it. Afterwards, the boa went to pass through a "V" opening at the bottom of a tree. He found he couldn't continue because of the bulge caused by the rabbit he had just eaten! He was about to back out when, to his surprise, another tasty rabbit appeared. The snake quickly disposed of the second rabbit.

Unfortunately, the boa was unable to go forward because of the first rabbit lump in his tail section and unable to go back because of the second rabbit in his front section. The boa began to whine and fume because of this cruel twist of fate. He stewed and fretted about his unfortunate situation, perhaps feeling he was a poor victim of circumstance. In reality, he was not a victim. He was addicted to rabbits. He had simply taken on more than he could possibly chew!

Like the boa constrictor, we can take on more than we can handle, which can bind us down to mediocrity. When we attempt to do everything, something must suffer. Though our intentions are pure, the results are the same. No one can do everything, perfectly.

Many women feel both internal and external pressure to be Superwoman! They have grown up with the impression that they can and should do it all. Unfortunately, no one can do it all—even when you give your best efforts. We have seen many women struggle under the weight of everything that they feel they must do. Interestingly, others who are close to these women are often unaware of the distress and exhaustion. Why? Because a Superwoman does not need help and cannot exhibit flaws, weakness, or needs. Their job is to keep everyone else functioning, and there is no provision in their thinking that allows them to receive help from others; they help others!

Jane falls into this category. She is forty years old, a mother of seven, with a husband who is constantly busy with work and church. She is concerned about his well-being and the individual difficulties of her children. She is also concerned about the mental health of other family members and the stress and strain of them taking on more. So what does Jane do? She picks up the slack. She doesn't want to add to her husband's or children's stress, so she does everything herself. She would never think of asking for help and only occasionally does she complain when she begins to be crushed under the massive weight of her many responsibilities. Yet she won't give up. Jane pushes on and on and on.

Unfortunately, Jane can't continue this way. In counseling, she has acknowledged that life is too painful and hard, so she attempts to avoid stress by cutting corners, becoming less emotionally or physically available, or sleeping. Unaware of Jane's pain, those around her go on. In fact, many of her friends and neighbors see her as a pillar of strength and often ask about her secrets to success. Many would be shocked if they knew she has considered running away to escape this unrelenting life and even entertained fleeting thoughts of suicide.

Several things could help Jane. First, she must recognize that there is no such thing as Superwoman. Second, she should ask for help when stressed beyond her limits. Asking for assistance is a sign of mental health, not weakness. Third, she must recognize she's could be preventing the growth and development of others when she does too much for them. Fourth, if worst comes to worst, she can let things go until she regains some emotional and physical strength and feels strong enough to resume her previous level of activity. (Suggested strategies: 4, 6, 10,11, 13, 15, 16, 21, 24, 29)

Awareness

Where am I? Where do I want to be?

Directions: Below are descriptions of each barrier extreme. Read them and then circle the number where you think you are. Feel free to ask for feedback from a spouse or close friends and associates. Remember: Zero signifies balance (our goal). Are you too far on the directionless side or too far on the congested side? Where would you rather be?

DIRECTIONLESS		CONGESTED
I feel like I am wandering around with little or nothing to do much of the time. I don't know where I am going, and I am not finding life very interesting. It is difficult to find something that is exciting or that I would like to do.	54321**0**12345	I have committed myself to too many things at the present time. It is difficult to concentrate on what I am doing because my mind goes from one thing to another, and I don't have enough time and energy for my commitments.

TOO RESPONSIBLE ⟷ IRRESPONSIBLE

Responsible

Description:

These individuals feel inordinately bad or guilty if they make a mistake or even think they have made a mistake. In addition, they take extreme responsibility for anything that goes wrong. Taking such extreme responsibility leads to overwhelming guilt. Individuals wracked by this guilt harbor feelings of hopelessness, discouragement, and despair. They feel they are unworthy of help or forgiveness.

Discussion:

It is important to recognize and accept the difference between rational and irrational guilt. Individuals who have rational guilt recognize when they have done something wrong and feel bad about it. In other words, the guilt they feel motivates them to compensate for what they have done wrong. Those who have irrational guilt feel more than reasonable guilt for things they have said or done, and for things for which they have little or no responsibility.

Reasonable guilt can be a powerful motivator to change and improve our thoughts and behavior. Excessive guilt becomes a heavy burden that negatively affects the way we think, feel, and act. It weighs us down and paralyzes our desires and abilities to do and be better. Such guilt is unproductive and often dangerous. Excessive and irrational guilt develops into discouragement, and in the grasp of discouragement, our progress is retarded and perhaps blocked.

Guilt is frequently accompanied by depression and anxiety. It accumulates exponentially and crushes us under a mass of a self-inflicted burden. Depressed people tend to live in the past, wishing they had done things differently. Their favorite question is, "If only?" Anxious people, on the other hand, tend to dwell in the future, wondering and worrying about what it will bring. Their favorite question is, "What if?" Healthy people learn from the past, prepare for the future, and live in the present. Balance is a major key in effectively dealing with the past and the future.

To some a feeling of guilt is a form of penance, suggesting that "the guiltier I feel, the more forgiven I will be." They often feel that by feeling guilty they are doing something about their unwanted thoughts and behaviors.

People who are racked with guilt often feel unworthy of help from others. They feel that friendship and forgiveness are for everyone but them because "I am too bad."

Ned was raised as an only child by his father and given everything imaginable. The two of them were famously happy. Unfortunately, Ned lost his father to a tragic and early death. Ned was devastated, and his aunt and uncle took him in. Ned appreciated their willingness to provide for him, but his life was never the same. He felt as if he inconvenienced them. Because of these feelings, Ned left their home as soon as he became of age. He entered the military and learned skills that are generally frowned upon in society. One of these skills was his ability to "scrounge" stuff he needed. Ned was viewed as a "guy who would get the job done" by his superiors and peers and was rewarded for this creativity while in the military.

In the civilian world, however, his scrounging skill was not appreciated. He experienced a constant urge to take things he didn't have from those who would never miss it. He would never consider stealing from the poor but rationalized that the rich could afford to "donate" certain items.

Ned married and had several children. As the children grew, his ability to provide for them was challenged. His view of himself as a good provider was in jeopardy, and because providing for his family was a high priority to him, he felt inadequate. Unfortunately, he often resorted to his earlier habit of scrounging, taking things that didn't belong to him. The less adequate he felt, the greater the temptation to steal. The combination of his illegal behavior with his feelings of not being able to provide for his family like he wanted caused Ned to feel even worse about himself. This, of course, led to a lower sense of worth, and his resulting frustration was often taken out on his wife and family. The children grew, and the older children married and became upstanding citizens in their respective communities. Ned's relationship with his wife and the younger children worsened, and he and his wife eventually separated. Ned moved into his own apartment and continued to work, attempting to regain his former financial state. He sought to see his family whenever possible. Living alone and without his wife and family, he began to recognize how his years of dishonesty, lies, alcohol use, and anger had driven a wedge between himself and his wife and younger children. He began to see himself for what he was: a sinner.

He felt hopeless. He knew that no matter what he did, he could never reclaim his wife and family. He felt personal responsibility for saving himself and could not bring himself to rely on others. He was about to give up when a friend gave him a talk tape, to which he listened repeatedly as he drove to and from work. Ned accepted his guilt and began to make decisions that would help him put his life back into balance. He began changing many of his old habits. He came to understand his basic self-worth, which created a glimmer of light at the end of his hopeless tunnel.

Ned continues to struggle with his self-esteem, and his family continues to question his motives, but he has hope! He realizes his efforts are not in vain and are appreciated by those closest to him. Slowly his depression is lifting. He recognizes he has a long, arduous journey ahead of him, but he knows the results will be worth the effort. (Suggested strategies: 4, 6, 8, 13, 14, 17, 19, 21, 23, 26, 27, 29)

Irresponsible
Description:

Extremely irresponsible individuals are selfish. Unless something pertains directly to them, they simply don't care. They are often desensitized and give little or no thought to the impact of their behavior. Such individuals are scary to be around. They lack ethics, boundaries, and limits, which leaves little to govern their thoughts and behaviors. Because they have no apparent conscience, they are unpredictable and cannot be trusted, even by those close to them.

Discussion:

Because irresponsible individuals have no regrets, they are not motivated to change and seldom learn from past mistakes. They care little or not at all about the effect their attitudes or behaviors have on others. They feel forced to do what they do because others deserve to be treated this way. This would be the case with a wife abuser who maintains that if his wife had not done whatever, he would not have hit her. Somehow it is always someone else's fault.

Take Jack, a shoplifter. Jack maintained he was forced into his illegal actions. He felt strongly that he was not receiving enough welfare assistance. He suggested that he wouldn't have had to shoplift if he were given more to live on. He felt he had no choice but to steal because others hadn't provided for his needs and wants. When this illogical and external thinking occurs, behavior is nearly impossible to change. (Suggested strategies: 5, 13, 21, 27, 29)

An individual's social indifference or lack of conscience often stems from an extreme or misguided loyalty to someone or something in which they believe. They are loyal to the point that nothing else matters. Many examples exist of individuals who innocently join such a cause because of their beliefs or the beliefs of others. At some point, however, a pathological change occurs.

Pete is one of the most impressive cases of extreme irresponsibility I've seen. The police brought thirteen-year-old Pete to the psychiatric unit in hand and foot shackles. I met with him the next day knowing only bits of the experiences that resulted in his admission to our unit. I introduced myself and asked why he was in the hospital. Initially, he claimed he didn't know, but when I told him that people are not generally admitted to the hospital, especially in a locked unit, for no reason, he reluctantly admitted that he and his buddy had broken into several cars. I asked why he had done this, and he noted that when he was angry, he could reduce his anger if he could "break something." The police report indicated that he and his friend were so angry that they had broken the windshields of more than one hundred cars.

As I explored Pete's thinking, I was amazed at his lack of conscience or remorse for his behaviors. "If they [referring to the victims] didn't want their cars broken into," he said, "they should have put the cars in the garage where no one could get to them." He blamed his actions on others.

If Pete amazed me, his mother was equally astonishing. When I spoke to her, she claimed that her son was a "good boy" and the doctors and society were at fault. She said that Pete was having difficulties because he had been labeled in a negative way by society, including the police, doctors, car owners, etc. It quickly became apparent that Pete had developed such extreme personal irresponsibility by following the example and teaching of his mother. (Suggested strategies: 5, 8, 13, 21, 28, 29)

Awareness

Where am I? Where do I want to be?

Directions: Below are descriptions of each barrier extreme. Read them and then circle the number where you think you are. Feel free to ask for feedback from a spouse or close friends and associates. Remember: Zero signifies balance (our goal). Are you too far on the responsible side or too far on the irresponsible side? Where would you rather be?

RESPONSIBLE		IRRESPONSIBLE
I often feel responsible in one way or another if anything goes wrong. I feel bad when I make a mistake.	5 4 3 2 1 **0** 1 2 3 4 5	It is difficult for me to accept any responsibility or feel guilt for things that go wrong because I don't really care. It's not my concern or responsibility. I tend to blame others.

DISORGANIZED ←——→ ORGANIZED

Disorganized
Description:

Many individuals who struggle with disorganization and confusion maintain that the problem is an inherited trait that they cannot control. Often they use their disorganization as an excuse rather than an explanation for their lack of success. They always seem to find somebody or something to blame for their difficulties. This attitude generally impedes their progress toward their potential. For example, disorganized people can spend so much valuable time and energy searching through their clutter, they seldom complete a task, much less do a good job when they do complete one. Relative to the hula hooping skills available to these individuals, coordination is extremely difficult and concentration is often not present or even in the picture.

Discussion:

As you can imagine, disorganization is not only found on cluttered desks or tabletops, but in our minds as well. Disorganized individuals, as well as those around them, are generally frustrated and stressed. For example, when we are running late, our stress builds as we hunt for our car keys. Others find it difficult to confide in and trust someone who is constantly distracted, disorganized, and confused. Others often feel it is easier to do things themselves, rather than trust a disorganized individual to get things together.

It is Saturday afternoon at the Murphy home. The baby is not feeling well and has developed a fever. Pam Murphy asks her husband, Jack, to go into town for some medicine.

Jack heads for the car only to discover a flat tire. His tools are in the other garage, and he goes to get them. As he enters the tool room he sees that the cat has spilled a bucket of nails on the floor. Worried about a possible accident, Jack gets his broom and begins cleaning up the mess. As he is sweeping, he notices a nest of spiders. He drops the broom and heads for the garden storage shed, where he has a special spray insecticide for spiders and other insects.

Finding the insect spray, his eye catches sight of an exposed electrical wire. Afraid he will forget to fix it, he puts the spray can down and heads back to the tool room for electrical tape and wire cutters. As he is about to leave the room, the phone rings. He picks up the phone and becomes totally involved in the conversation. After the call, which is quite lengthy, he heads back inside to talk to his wife.

As he walks in, his wife asks him for the medicine.

Jack races back to the car, removes the flat tire, puts on the spare, and speeds into town. As he approaches the store door, he sees a sign notifying customers that the pharmacist is out of town and the store will reopen on Monday at 10 a.m. There is nothing Jack can do but go home and face his wife and sick child. He had meant well, but Jack hadn't accomplished anything of real importance.

This made-up story is not so far off the mark. Many people suffer from such extreme disorganization. Ruth struggles with this area of unbalance. She has so many wonderful talents and attributes, yet this one area continues to frustrate her; she is not nearly as productive as she wants to be. Ruth is a bright, capable forty-year-old homemaker. Her children and her husband are her top priorities.

As a mother, Ruth made a goal to always be home when her children were home. When they were young, she remained home with them. As they grew and attended school, she was always there when they left for school and when they returned from school. The first person they looked for when they came in the door was Mom. Ruth loved to share the day's activities with them. She expressed joy and excitement at the new experiences they had, sympathy on those rare bad days, and love every day.

Ruth's biggest enemies were her disorganization, confusion, and feelings of being overwhelmed. She would begin one project, like the laundry, and the phone would ring. The phone call distracted her, so when she finished her call, she moved to another activity, such as cleaning the bathroom. However, something else would interrupt her, and she never seemed to complete any task. As her tasks piled up, she felt overwhelmed and paralyzed.

Ruth rarely had a schedule or list to guide her activities. As a result, she was always behind and frustrated by her inability to maintain the house. With some organization, structure, and routine, Ruth could have moved to a better level of balance and removed her ever-present frustration, anxiety, and guilt. (Suggested strategies: 2, 9, 13, 24, 26, 28, 30)

Organized
Description:

Compulsive people are often controlled by their need for organization rather than controlling their organization. Their compulsion often takes on a life of its own, and life centers on their need for organization and neatness. They spend more time organizing things than they do completing things. Compulsive individuals proceed with little or no regard for potential results because they are so rigid and task focused. Compulsive people work from a "must do" orientation rather than a "want to" premise. Consequently, they are weighed down with tasks and details which, if not real, are personally manufactured.

These people are often driven by "shoulds," "musts," and "oughts." Family, friends, and associates often perceive compulsive individuals as robots rather than caring and concerned human beings. In a compulsive person's world, rules and order are supreme and more important than people and feelings.

Discussion:

Compulsive people tend to get caught up in "the thick of thin things."[1] As a result, they lose sight of what is most important and fail to maintain the main thing as the main thing. Because they are so focused on their compulsion, compulsive individuals are frequently considered self-centered and insensitive to the needs and desires of those around them; they are slaves to their self-imposed need for organization, order, and control.

Compulsive people are difficult to be around, and others often seek distance from them. Often compulsive individuals are driven to distraction and a point of self-destruction if they fail to measure up to their excessively high expectations and standards. Frustration results from unfulfilled expectations; consequently, those who are extremely compulsive are almost always in a state of frustration and discomfort.

An attractive, intelligent, capable woman, Nancy sought therapy when her second marriage ended in divorce. She couldn't understand why her latest husband had pursued a divorce, yet she felt like the death of her marriage was completely her fault. Her goal in therapy was to discover what was driving others away.

During our initial visit, it became apparent that Nancy was an extremely organized individual, obsessed with cleanliness and orderliness. She could not tolerate any disruption in her rigid, structured agenda. Everyone in her family had a "honey do" list, and they were not allowed to relax until the items on that list were completed—to Nancy expectations. Within minutes of returning home from work, Nancy would wash dishes, straighten pictures, rearrange magazines on the coffee table, clean counters, and readjust furniture to a precise position. Nancy didn't allow playing in the house because she couldn't tolerate any mess, clutter, or lack of structure.

Nancy felt guilt if every spare minute wasn't spent doing something productive. With her extremely high aspirations, she expected perfection from herself, her children, and her spouse. Without recognizing it, Nancy harassed and belittled family members who disrupted her perfect home. As a result of her extreme sense of order, her second marriage dissolved.

After her second divorce, Nancy developed feelings of self-loathing and depression. In her mind, she was at fault for her two failed marriages.

Her attitudes toward order and perfectionism carried over into the workplace. Initially, Nancy's friends and associates considered her one of the kindest, most thoughtful individuals—until they began to see her rigid behaviors, which squeezed all the fun out of life. They noticed that she became so preoccupied with order, rules, and results that she never had time for fun or enjoyment.

Fortunately, Nancy entered therapy with an open mind, motivated to change. Nancy is learning how to relax and become better balanced in her home and work life. As a result, she is growing closer to her children and finds more enjoyment and contentment in life. She is the first to recognize that she still has much to work on, yet she can clearly see the benefits of obtaining balance in her life. (Suggested strategies: 1, 4, 6, 10, 13, 17, 18, 24, 26, 28, 30)

Awareness

Where am I? Where do I want to be?

Directions: Below are descriptions of each barrier extreme. Read them and then circle the number where you think you are. Feel free to ask for feedback from a spouse or close friends and associates. Remember: Zero signifies balance (our goal). Are you too far on the disorganized side or too far on the organized side? Where would you rather be?

DISORGANIZED		ORGANIZED
I can never find things when I need them. Things are extremely messy around my workstation; I find it difficult to get things done.	5 4 3 2 1 **0** 1 2 3 4 5	I must have things in neat order. When they are not, I feel I will lose my mind. I often spend more time organizing things than actually working on them.

Note

1. Marion D. Hanks, *Speeches of the Year* (quoting Edith Wharton), May 28, 1964, 110.

Section IV

Strategies for Obtaining and Maintaining Balance

Once a diagnosis has been made and explained to our patients, many of them look at us and say something along the lines of, "I already knew that. What I want to know is what to do about it. How can I change?"

Many individuals become frustrated with psychotherapy because they feel there is too much "insight" offered and too few step-by-step suggestions about how to change. The primary focus of this section is to offer specific suggestions and strategies for making desired changes in both attitude and behavior. Remember, however, that diagnosis must precede prescription. In other words, we must first determine where we are and where we want to be before choosing a strategy to get there.

The ability to successfully participate in a hula-hoop experience is a learned rather than an inherited skill. It requires an understanding of basic dynamics, perseverance, and the practice of specific skills. The specific skills offered here can only help establish and maintain balance when someone chooses to know them and do them.

Several years ago, during CB's early years of teaching, an associate made a profound, if not slightly funny, statement. He was addressing teachers and administrators, encouraging them to at least try to reach out and touch each student who might come into their classes. His statement went like this: "There is a wrench for every nut in the world." CB knew he wasn't talking about shopping in a hardware store.

We are unique in our personality and environment; no two individuals are exactly alike. Even identical twins growing up in the same household do not share identical experiences. Because of inherent differences, there is not one cure for all ills, nor one adjustment strategy that enables every searching person to reach balance. With that in mind, we want to share several options and encourage you to choose which strategy works best for you in your pursuit of balance.

We will provide these strategies in alphabetical order with a brief explanation about each one.

Act as If—and You Can Become (1)

The initial step of this strategy is writing a specific description of the balance you would like to achieve. Ask yourself questions like "What would I want to say?" "How would I like to say it?"" "How would I like to look?" "What would I like to do?" Then answer them in as much detail as possible. Once the description has been written, the strategy is to act as if you had already achieved this balance.

Perry tried this strategy. Perry loved to hide from those who loved him by immersing himself in his computer work and magazine articles. In Perry's case, this method did not work well because he was not motivated to be anything other than what he was. He wrote out a description, but it was a description of what he thought his wife wanted him to become. Had he been motivated to change, we think this strategy would have facilitated his adjustment.

Desiring a personal change is paramount for any of the strategies we will present. At one point, CB was working with Irene, the unhappy wife of a well-known faculty member at a university. Irene wasn't really dissatisfied with her husband or her children, but she definitely didn't like herself, or at least her perception of herself. CB asked her to describe, in as much detail as she could, the type of wife, mother, and woman she would like to be; we began by asking the questions listed above.

Although it took significant effort, Irene answered the questions, even writing the description down in considerable detail. We met a week or so later. After sharing and discussing her description, we chose to apply the "Act As If" principle and strategy. Here is what we did and how it was done.

The entire family drove to the airport, pretending to send Irene on a one-month vacation to Hawaii. Irene would be gone for thirty days and have no contact with her husband and four children. Once at the airport, she walked into the women's restroom as if she were boarding the aircraft; her family even hugged and kissed her before she left, and waved goodbye to her as she disappeared through the restroom door.

About ten minutes later, she reappeared, dressed in clothing that fit the person she wanted to become. She even had a new name; she joined her family as Aunt Alice, the embodiment of the person she wanted to become. She was there to take care of the family for the next thirty days while Irene was in Hawaii. Her husband and children actually called her Aunt Alice as she played this role for a month.

To make a long story short, after thirty days of role playing, the family returned to airport; they sent Aunt Alice away and welcomed Irene home. During the thirty-day period, Irene had tried to act in the manner she desired, and according to all participants, she had done a wonderful job. She had dressed, talked, worked, played, and even sang the way she had envisioned herself.

Irene reported that this was a difficult but rewarding assignment. She didn't become the new person, but she did experience significant changes that she thoroughly enjoyed and vowed to maintain in her real self. Her husband indicated that her change bordered on the miraculous.

Once Irene made initial changes, she needed to pace herself as she sought to incorporate the positive changes into her life. In this strategy, coordination with Irene's family was critical and continuous motion was imperative. If Irene stopped her changes, the hoop would fall to her ankles and she would find herself back where she started.

Most people who try this strategy feel it is too difficult to do twenty-four/seven but find success acting for one- to two-hour periods. If you choose this approach, act as if you are on a stage or in a movie with the cameras rolling. You will likely be surprised by the positive feedback you receive from those around you as you approach balance. The more comfortable you and those around you are with your efforts, the easier it will be for you to continue living in balance. You may not reach perfect balance, but you will surely end up closer to where you would like to be. Remember, rewarded behavior continues.

Act on It (2)

We have stated this previously but repeat the statement here for emphasis. ***If nothing changes, nothing will change.*** Sounds simple enough, doesn't it? Apply this concept to whatever feedback you might receive from others or even from yourself relative to the specific behavior you have chosen to focus on in your attempt to achieve balance. Knowing something is the first step, but you need to devote your energy, insights, and wisdom to doing something if you want to enjoy the benefits that come with balance.

Matthew repeatedly indicated his desire to change the way he interacted with others, especially his wife, but he was never able to translate his spoken words into actions. Week after week, he apologized for not completing the assignments he received in counseling, and week after week, he recommitted to changing his behavior. Sadly, he did not act on the suggestions, and his wife and children left him.

Even if what you try doesn't work the way you thought it would, you have at least learned what doesn't work. Knowing this, you avoid wasting your energies on certain strategies again. If what you attempt works, you can do it more often. However, keep in mind that some things that work well for a while may begin to be less effective as time goes on. You actions may become routine. You must remain open to new adventures and approaches, making adjustments when necessary, keeping in mind always that the central idea is to do something. You cannot expect something to change if nothing is changed.

Another Perspective (3)

Occasionally we can look at something so long that we lose sight of what we are actually seeing. It is possible that we won't even recognize our own unbalance, but that those around us will.

One strategy that has worked for many out-of-balance individuals is to view their situation from a different vantage point. In therapy, we call this "reframing," because you take a picture out of one frame and place it in a different one. In most cases, the picture looks different.

Some time ago, I counseled a woman who told me she couldn't pay her fee. She was the mother of some good friends, and I agreed to see her without compensation. The counseling went well, and when she arrived for her final session, she gave me a painting she had done herself. The painting itself was nice; however, she'd framed it in a black frame, which made the picture look dark. In addition, the frame didn't match the oak furniture I had in my office.

I made this observation, and she agreed, taking the painting with her when she left. She returned the painting a few days later, this time in a beautiful oak frame. Complemented by this new frame, the painting looked beautiful and matched my office décor perfectly. I was astonished how different the picture looked in the new frame.

So it is with many of life's situations. Things can look very ominous when viewed from one perspective; however, when we look at it from another point of view, it doesn't appear nearly as threatening.

This strategy helped Mitchell deal with his adjustment into civilian life. After some discussion, he realized how detrimental it would be to continue viewing his life from a military point of view. Although it was difficult for him to change his perspective, things went much better once he made the adjustment. Seeing his current associates in a different light allowed him to adjust his expectations of them, and this action reduced his frustration.

Look at the behavior or attitude you are trying to change. For example, you may want to think about how your children view your behavior. Once you consider things from their viewpoint, you may find yourself motivated to move in a different direction, a direction that helps you come closer to balance.

Ask the Right Questions (4)

Several years ago I found myself extremely frustrated with what was happening in my life. I had fallen out of balance with my chosen occupation. While I loved what I did, I wanted more than it was providing. I was discussing this situation with an internist friend of mine during an appointment. I asked him if he thought I ought to change professions to fulfill my current dreams. We talked about several different job possibilities. Suddenly, he said, "I think you are asking yourself the wrong question."

"What do you mean?" I queried in return.

"Well," he continued, "it seems to me you are struggling over whether or not to change careers at this stage in your life."

"That's right," I agreed. "I am."

Placing his stethoscope around his neck, he said, "I think it's the wrong question."

I told him to keep talking. "Your question shouldn't be about changing one occupation for another," he observed, "but rather how to incorporate your new dreams with what you already have. If you are able to combine them, you can retain your security and all the positive elements of what you are currently doing without risking more than you are willing to lose."

What he said made perfect sense to me, and my frustration disappeared.

I felt more in balance than I had for some time. It is interesting how we can become so embroiled in our own circumstances that we fail to see a way out of it.

Sometimes a change in the questions we are asking may lead to better answers.

Another example of asking different questions is found in the book *When Bad Things Happen to Good People,* by Rabbi Harold S. Kushner.[1] In his book, Rabbi Kushner talked about his son who was suffering from progeria and growing old much too soon; in fact, doctors warned he would not likely live past twenty years of age. Beset with grief, concern, and confusion, the rabbi spent quite a long time asking questions like, "Why is this happening to us?"

The rabbi was trying to determine a cause or fix blame on someone, anyone, but his confusion and frustration pushed him out of balance. To me, the primary thesis of the book is his personal discovery that the "Why?" questions are the wrong questions.

His own discovery suggests that a better question to ask might be, "What can I learn from this experience?" rather than trying to determine why the experience happened. Changing the question alters our focus and helps us regain our balance.

Sometimes simply asking ourselves different questions can clear up our thinking about unbalances. Remember Jane, who was trying to be Superwoman and becoming more and more worn out. Had she stopped at some point during her impossible daily schedule and asked herself a few questions abut what was going on in her life at that moment, she may have discovered that her uncomfortable feelings were directly tied to her trying to function so far out of balance. Questions like: "What is happening to me?" "Is what I am doing getting me to where I want to go?" and "Is this the way I want to live the rest of my life?" may have helped her discover valuable strategies for getting out of the rat race in which she found herself.

Try asking yourself pointed and direct questions, such as:

- Where will I end up if I continue doing what I am doing?
- What would the Lord want me to do?
- Where do I want to be in ten years?

You might be surprised at the answers, answers that will motivate you to regain balance.

Attitude Analysis (5)

Earlier we discussed an experience during which a young girl handed out a card to classmates attending a classroom discussion. On the card was written: So often we seek a change in our condition when what we really need is a change in our attitude.

This strategy suggests that we step back and closely examine our attitudes about the circumstances that are causing or contributing to our feeling out of balance. Along with attitudes, we may want to look at expectations as well; unrealistic expectations can also lead to feelings of unbalance. Many individuals come back into balance simply by challenging and eventually changing their attitudes and expectations.

We are not certain that Pete was mature enough to analyze his attitudes about life, but if he could, this idea would be a workable treatment strategy for him. As long as he continues to blame others for his misdeeds, he will be unmotivated to change his behavior. Somehow he needs to realize that with his self-serving attitude, he is headed for jail or similar uncomfortable circumstances.

In analyzing your attitude, you might ask yourself the following questions:

- What is it about this situation that bothers me so much?
- Is there another way to view this situation?
- If so, what is it?
- What do I think I can gain from maintaining my current attitude?
- What will I lose if I continue thinking and feeling the way I presently do?
- How long has this attitude been part of my life?
- Is my current attitude helping me reach my goals or is it blocking my progress?
- Am I holding someone else responsible for my condition?
- If so, whom and why do I think this?
- How critical is this situation, really?
- Would I die if things didn't work out or would it just be inconvenient?

You'll find it is often helpful to step back and look at our own attitudes, analyzing them and adjusting them when needed. This approach is far more effective than blaming others for our unbalance. Remember, thoughts and attitudes determine actions.

Comparisons: Some Are Good and Some Are Not (6)

To suggest using comparisons as a strategy for regaining a sense of balance may sound peculiar because comparisons are often a major cause of unbalance. Key to this approach is making comparisons that motivate us to change. The most common comparison, the one that pushes many off balance, occurs when we compare our worst or least attractive traits with the best or most attractive traits of others. When we make this comparison, we are destined to end up with the short end of the stick.

One example of just such a destructive comparison would be the young mother who feels inadequate because her home does not stay as clean as her neighbor's home. The young mother has five children under the age of ten; her neighbor has two teenagers who are seldom at home. This is an unfair comparison. Every feeling of inferiority is the result of a faulty comparison.

One of the primary motivators for Ramona's spending unbalance was her habit of constantly looking at what her friends and neighbors had; their homes, clothes, recreational toys, and vacations. Interestingly, she never examined how much she and her husband had compared to people who lived in smaller homes and in neighborhoods whose yards did not house boats or camping vehicles. Oh, no, she only compared her possessions with those who had more.

On the other hand, we can find value in comparing ourselves with ourselves. Setting a goal to become perfect in this life is not realistic; however, setting our sights on achieving excellence is. Excellence can be measured by comparing our current position on the path to excellence with where we were a year, a month, or even a week ago. A sense of progress encourages a greater sense of balance in our efforts to progress.

We may experience another constructive comparison when we look at where we have been compared to where we are going. Have you ever noticed how much shorter a long trip seems when we look back to where we came from rather than looking ahead to how far we have to go? This consideration worked wonders with our small children when we were traveling long distances. Such a realization provides a sense of balance.

Several years ago, I read an advertisement that has come to my aid many times. I do not recall many details of the ad, but the caption has remained forever present in my mind. It read: Better than yesterday, not as good as tomorrow. This manner of thinking is a wonderful example of a constructive comparison, which provides hope and encourages us to move towards personal improvement and greater balance.

The strategy of constructive comparisons also suggests that when we sense an imbalance in our lives, we might identify any unfair comparisons we might be making. Having identified the source, we can reevaluate our thinking and behavior relative to our goal and make any needed alterations to regain balance. Jeff would have felt better much sooner had he recognized his propensity to compare himself with his personally created, ideal self-image. As long as he insisted on achieving the impossible, he experienced lower feelings of self-worth.

As you can see, the act of comparing is a two-edged sword. If used incorrectly it can throw us off balance, but if used productively it can help us regain peace and harmony.

Consider the Source (7)

We cannot count the number of counseling sessions we have conducted with individuals who have been thrown off balance because of what someone said or insinuated. The truth is that someone thinking, saying, or doing something does not make what they are thinking, saying, or doing fact. Individuals view life from their own perspective and many times what they are experiencing has little to do with what might be going on in us. The strategy, to consider the source, suggests that we do not automatically accept what we hear or see as our personal reality. We gain much balance if we do not react too quickly to what we hear, but rather wait until we have verified information. When we understand the source and motive, then we can decide to give credence to the information or ignore it.

For example, Ann swallowed, as truth, everything her mother told her. And from the description of her mother's explanations and demands, it was clear that the mother was the one who was out of balance. Just because we *think* we are right, doesn't necessarily make us right!

Decisions Determine Direction and Destiny (8)

How many decisions do you make during any given day? Too many to count, especially if you include smaller, inconsequential ones like which pair of white socks to wear and whether to brush your hair or teeth first. This strategy is based upon the concept that an unbalanced condition is caused by decisions made by ourselves and those around us. And if certain decisions cause unbalance, it makes sense that other decisions can cause balance.

Jonathan's decision to not make decisions was a real impediment to a balanced life. Balance can be reestablished in our lives when we make good decisions in a constructive manner.

One couple had a terrible time deciding what to do for their date nights. This indecisiveness often led to arguments and an uncomfortable loss of balance between them. All too frequently they ended up canceling everything, staying at home, and harboring ill feelings towards each other.

This date night dilemma is not difficult to solve. One solution might be to have each person take five pieces of paper and write down an appealing date night activity on each piece of paper. After each person has written on the slips of paper, fold each piece of paper and place them in a bowl or hat. When the next date night arrives, draw one of the alternatives out of the hat. The date activity is decided, and specific plans can be made. (Note: you want to make certain that the suggested activities are within your time and money resources and will not cause either person to compromise personal standards.)

One night, CB and his wife went out to dinner; they planned to attend a theater production afterwards. Unfortunately, neither one felt very well during dinner, but neither wanted to say anything to the other because neither didn't want to spoil the evening and miss the show. After dessert they looked at each other and said, "Let's do it by the numbers."

Doing it by the numbers means that they pound their fists on the table three times, and on the third pound, they expose one to five fingers on the table. Five fingers means the person really wants to continue whatever it is they're doing, in this case attending the show. One finger meant the person wants to go home. Of course, each person must expose his or her fingers at the same time. Their personal rule with this approach to decision making is that if the combined total score equals six or more, they continue. If the total equals less than six, they head for home. On this particular night, their total was four, so they went home.

Some people flip coins to make similar decisions; others play Rock, Paper, Scissors. As you work to maintain balance in your lives and make decisions that aren't critical, have fun and honor the results whether or not you like them.

Have you ever sensed that someone you cared a lot about was out of balance, but you didn't know for sure? One way to evaluate how others are feeling is to ask them a question and then suggest they choose a number from one to ten that indicates how strongly they feel about the question. The number ten might indicate strong feelings, while a number closer to zero indicates feelings that aren't as strong or favorable.

For example, one night CB son arrived home from a basketball game. When asked how things had gone, he replied, "Is there anything lower than zero?" The question had been answered, and the son received the comfort and encouragement he needed.

On another occasion, CB walked into his office and noticed a member of his staff sitting with her head on her desk. CB asked how she was doing. "About a five," she answered.

"And which way is the number heading?" CB followed up.

"Down," came the reply. In less than ten minutes, she was on her way home to rest and recuperate.

What we are trying to suggest is that many times an unbalance can be rectified by implementing methods of making decisions or gathering information that create unity rather than foster dividedness. The methods suggested above can be both fun and productive. And, of course, they don't have to be limited to the examples we've provided. The next time you are faced with a decision you cannot harmoniously make, try one of these strategies and stay in balance. Of the five hooping skills, control is one of the most significant.

Do More of What Works (9)

If individuals sense they are out of balance, they are able to do so because they are comparing what they are feeling with what they felt when things were going better.

The key to this approach is to think about what you were doing or saying when you were in balance, and then replicate that experience. The basis for this suggestion is that if it worked once it should work again.

Those who have experienced success with a hula hoop in the past feel much more frustrated with their inability to hula hoop than do those who have not tasted much success with the toy. Those who have been successful want to repeat what has worked for them, and when they fail to do so, frustration mounts.

Eighteen-year-old Charlene complained that she hadn't been able to confide in her father for over two years and desperately wanted to do so again. They had been in balance with one another two years earlier, she reported. CB had her think back to the last time she and her father had had a good heart-to-heart talk with one another. "Remember where you were, what you were doing, and what the environment was like," CB told her.

After some coaxing and prodding, she was able to recall that experience along with several other times she and her father had had meaningful, sensitive conversations. After she had discussed these earlier experiences, CB asked her to compare the conditions that existed then with what currently happened when the two of them attempted to talk seriously with one another. The differences became very clear to her, and she vowed to return home and approach her father as she had those years before.

Later she reported that the plan had worked. She had dressed more modestly, approached her father right after dinner before he became involved in television, and used a sweet voice tone to convey her message. He responded as he had years earlier, and the two of them enjoyed a wonderful discussion.

Remembering things that have worked well for you in the past and repeating them generally helps you in achieving the balance you have lost.

Expectation Challenge (10)

Feelings of frustration are generally valid indicators of an unbalance in our lives, either within ourselves or between us and another person. Frustration results from unfulfilled expectations. This fact suggests that *our level of frustration or sense of unbalance is directly proportionate to the distance between what we expect and what we experience.* Therefore, the key to regaining your balance and reducing your frustration is to find ways to bring your expectations and experiences more closely in line. This suggests adjusting your expectation or altering your behavior in a positive way, or doing a little of both.

When we do not have control over what we experience, we must focus on adjusting our expectations if we want to regain our sense of balance. Identifying and challenging our expectations are the first two steps in making these adjustments and moving closer to balance.

Although it did not work extremely well, this is the approach Richard used in an attempt to help his family regain their balance and live more peaceful life. One of Richard's primary problems was that he expected others to view life as optimistically as he did. When they didn't do so, he felt frustrated. We discussed at great lengths the value of allowing others to view and react to the world as they perceived it. He agreed in theory but had a challenging time applying it in his family. When he did, he was less frustrated. When he did not, he was in trouble.

When we feel frustrated and out of balance, we can start by asking ourselves what it is we were expecting that isn't happening. Identifying our expectations is critical if we want to adjust them. Once we recognize our expectations, we need to challenge them. This process allows us to make the necessary adjustments.

The following questions have helped many of our patients challenge their expectations and adjust those expectations. This allows them to shrink the distance between what they expect and what they are experiencing, which naturally reduces their frustration. Pick and choose which questions will best assist you in understanding and altering the expectation you are focusing on.

- What am I actually expecting?
- What is the nature of my expectation?
- What is the origin of the expectation?
- Are things still the same as they were then?
- Is the expectation realistic?
- Is the expectation a generalization, or is it specific to this situation?
- Is the expectation significant enough at this particular time to warrant challenging?
- Is the expectation adjustable or is it an either/or situation?
- Is the expectation part of a larger expectation or does it stand alone?
- Is this expectation within my circle of control, so I am able to adjust it?
- Can this expectation be divided into smaller, more manageable units? If so, what might they be?
- What might happen if this expectation were adjusted downward?
- What impact might such an adjustment have on my world?

The primary purpose behind challenging an expectation is to decrease the distance between it and your experience. The more this occurs, the greater will be your sense of balance.

First Things First (11)

The hooping skills of coordination and concentration fit well into this strategy. Learning to prioritize the elements of our lives is one of the greatest skills we can learn. Only by determining what is most important to us and focusing on those things first can we feel a sense of accomplishment. When we make certain the important things are done, the less important ones seem to fall in place.

Many times we find ourselves out of balance simply because we are trying to do too many things. For example, Ruth was kidding herself when she thought she could do so many things. In fact, the more she tried to do, the less she was actually able to do. And what she did do, she didn't do as well as she hoped, which only increased her frustration. Had Ruth prioritized her many activities and duties, then accomplished only one thing, it would have been the most important thing in her life. This alone would have helped her feel better!

At the end of the day, people who are out of balance generally find themselves totally drained of energy and yet unable to think of anything they have accomplished. What could be more discouraging than that?

Zig Ziglar, a well-known motivational speaker, has said, "The main thing is to keep the main thing, the main thing." When we feel out of balance because we are working frantically to accomplish too many things, rethinking priorities can make a tremendous difference.

Of course, some people have never given much thought to what is most important in their lives. They may need help in recognizing their priorities. Of course, only we can determine our own priorities, but seeing what others' priorities are can be helpful. Marvin J. Ashton shares his priorities, which include the following:

1. To be a quality person.
2. To be a worthy companion.
3. To be a good mom or dad.
4. To be an attentive son or daughter.
5. To be a member of the church in good standing.
6. To be an effective leader.
7. To be a contributing member of society.[2]

Keep in mind that, once you establish your priorities, they may change as your life situations change. Failing to make adjustments can result in serious unbalance and discomfort. To illustrate this point, let's divide our lives into the following five segments:

- I (focus is primarily on self)
- Marriage (focus is on roles as husband or wife and the relationship between them)
- Family (focus is on our roles as a parent to our children, a parent partner to our spouse, and in the family as a unit)
- Work (focus is on our occupation, including being a student or homemaker)
- Other (focus is on such things as church, community, friends, etc.).

Each of these separate areas does not require the same amount of energy and focus. Prior to marriage, our primary focus is likely on the "I," while after marriage our relationship with our spouse needs greater attention. Once children enter the scene, the family role requires more focus, while the personal and even marriage roles may receive less attention, at least temporarily. Additionally, there are times, such as early in a career, where the job may require more time and energy than at other times.

Unbalance occurs when we try to focus all our energy in all five segments at all times. We must continually adjust our focus and redirect our energy in these various areas if we are to maintain peace and harmony.

When you first begin to bring your life into balance, write down your tasks and challenges, review them, and then rewrite them in a hierarchal order, listing the most important ones first. These areas are the ones that should receive your primary attention and efforts. If you create this prioritized list and are able to complete only *one* of the items, you will know that you have at least finished the most important one. This knowledge helps you feel more in balance.

Whenever an additional challenge comes into your life, repeat this exercise and rethink your priorities to make certain you are still working on your number one concern. Feeling in control is tantamount to feeling in balance.

How Am I Doing? (12)

This strategy is one of continuous motion, meaning we should never stop evaluating how we are doing. Feedback is essential in our goal of continuous course correction. Life goes on and so must we.

How many times have we heard someone say they couldn't see the forest because of the trees. When we ask others how we are doing, we recognize that we are often too close and too involved in situations and behaviors, and we need others' help as we work to regain and maintain balance. Often we might sense an unbalance, but because it is almost impossible to view personal situations with objectivity, we are unable to identify where we are and what we are doing to cause that unbalance.

This strategy would work exceptionally well in a situation like the one involving Dr. Jensen. A professional, Dr. Jensen was aware of his limitations and desired to overcome them. Those around him cared about him and were willing to help him. Their consistent answers to the question "How am I doing" could go a long way in helping this doctor reach a higher level of his potential.

We must have three basic characteristics to most effectively benefit from the input of others in our struggle for balance. First, we must have a strong **motivation** to ask for help. Second, we must be **willing to listen** to what others have to share. Third, we must be **open and accepting** of what they tell us.

This doesn't mean we need to do whatever others say without thinking about it, but we should ponder the input we receive and then choose actions that we feel will put us back on track. Obviously, the more we trust the individual, the more weight their feedback will carry. Being out of balance is not the time to allow personal pride to block us from the peace and harmony we seek.

If, Then (Anticipating Consequences) (13)

"If you pick up one end of the stick, you pick up the other end also. If you choose the beginning of a road, you choose also the destination to which it leads." CB remembers this "momilie" (something your mother told you when you were young) from his youth and it forms the basis for the If, Then strategy. This strategy suggests that we take a close look at our choices and determine where each choice might lead us. When adequately completed, this process can predict potential positive as well as negative consequences from any action choice.

Several years ago, a couple came in for marriage therapy. Jacob made the appointment after Monica asked for a divorce. They had been married for twelve years and had four young children.

On the surface, no one would have guessed that Monica was unhappy and dissatisfied. She had done some professional acting, and in her words, she had been playing the part of a dutiful wife and mother as if on a stage for the past several years but she was now at the point where she could no longer continue in the role. When pushed for the reasons behind her request for a divorce, all she could say was that she was "just not happy."

Jacob was beside himself. He loved Monica and felt his family was the most important thing in the world. In his mind, Monica had no justifiable reason to seek a divorce and split the family. Monica had agreed to counseling, although she did not want to try to explain to anyone what she was thinking. She accepted her state of confusion and felt that her life was out of balance but was uneasy exposing her inner thoughts and feelings to a stranger.

During counseling, it became clear that Monica had not considered many of the consequences connected with a divorce and its potential affect on everyone involved. That she was unhappy was obvious, as was the fact that something needed to change if the family was to stay together. The challenge was to help her understand the significance of her decision and to motivate her to reconsider, at least to the point of seriously considering all aspects. CB felt the marriage could be saved, even strengthened, and that Monica could find the joy and satisfaction she was seeking if she could discover and understand two things: first, the problems and concerns that generally follow a divorce, and second, the blessings and joy in her home and family.

CB suggested that Monica complete an "If, Then" exercise before proceeding with the divorce. She reluctantly agreed, even though in her mind the decision had been made.

This exercise consists of a diagram illustrating potential results for any decision we might make. The decision is written down, followed by an arrow that points to a possible result, which is followed by an arrow pointing to a potential outcome, which in turn might be followed by another arrow indicating another possible consequence.

Here is an abbreviated example of this strategy:

Should I change jobs? Yes → we would have to move → the children would have to change schools → it would give them a fresh start → they might try harder in their new surroundings → they would be more successful in their school work → and would love us for getting them out of an undesirable situation, and on and on and on.

If, on the other hand, the decision to change jobs was no, the exercise might look like this: No → the children would remain in the same school → they would be more comfortable but their current problems would continue → they would keep their same friendships, which have not been the best → they would miss their grandparents, who lived close to the location of the new job → but they could learn to appreciate their grandparents more when they visited, and on and on and on.

This exercise can be completed, or you can devote quite a bit of time to it. Monica accepted the challenge to work on an "If, Then" diagram and returned in two weeks with several pages of words and lines. She had clearly thought her situation over from several different angles and decided not to get a divorce, at least not at that time. She had made this decision not because she didn't want to divorce but because the potential cost was too high. She resolved to work on her relationship with Jacob and to keep the family together.

As we looked over her chart, she commented, "I knew what needed to be done, and the confusion and frustration left me once I realized all that would have been involved if I had gone through with what I had decided." Monica was on her way to regaining balance in her family relationships.

This strategy also worked for Mitchell. In one of our counseling sessions, CB asked him, "And if you did this, what would happen?" "If that happened, what would the outcome be?" "If that outcome occurred, what would the result be?" And on and on. He finally smiled and said he understood the technique.

Is It I? (14)

This three-word strategy has proven to be extremely helpful in assisting people regain balance. When we focus on ourselves and what we might do about a situation, we are dealing within the realm of possibilities. To focus on other people changing can be frustrating because we have no legitimate power or control over what others think or how they act.

Can you imagine the peace and harmony that would exist in a home or workplace where everyone was motivated to look inside for both the causes and cures of problems rather than attempting to blame someone else?

Martha, a woman about fifty years of age, visited CB looking for ways to get her husband, Jack, to stop arguing with her. In her mind, he argued about everything and always had to be right. She was extremely frustrated and unhappy and believed her husband was the one to blame. He was the one with the temper. He was the one who resorted to profanity and demeaning comments. He was the one who demonstrated no respect for the thoughts and opinions of others.

Jack refused to come in for counseling, and so the only individual CB could actually work with was Martha. CB began by asking Martha to look inward to determine how she might be contributing to the nonproductive communications at home. The general questions we reviewed were the following:

1. What can *I* do to reduce the tension?
2. What could *I* have done to avert this conflict situation?
3. How have *I* contributed to the present situation?
4. What are *my* current motives toward this situation?
5. What are *my* current feelings toward my spouse?
6. What part of this situation is *my* responsibility?
7. What can *I* do to demonstrate support for my spouse right now?
8. What did *I* do or say to leave the impression my spouse has?
9. Which part is *mine* to do apologize or forgive
10. How can *I* let my spouse know how much I love him or her?

The more we discussed Martha's responses to these questions, the greater insight she gained into her role in the relationship problems she brought to counseling. She began to recognize things she could do to reestablish peace and harmony in her marriage.

Remember Larry, who wanted to live life to the fullest and chose too many dangerous things? He was not willing to change his behavior and blamed his wife for her change in attitude since the birth of their child. In his mind, his wife was the primary reason for their marital problems. Because he refused to look at his own behavior, he was not motivated to change it.

Had he been willing to ask himself "Is it I?" or any of the questions listed above, he might have recognized his role in what was going wrong in the family, and his marriage might have been saved. Unfortunately, it was just too easy to point the finger of blame at his wife.

Not only does taking personal responsibility place us in an arena where we can actually do something, it removes or at least reduces the tension we have been creating in blaming others.

This "Is it I?" strategy has been summarized in the following poem:

Which Way Should I Point?
Should I point out or should I point in?
Sometimes I'm not sure just where to begin.
I'm too confused to know what's going on
Whatever it is, it's gone on much too long.
Is my finger made to point out at you?
Would pointing at me be better to do?
I go back and forth 'til I'm blue in the face
And when I stop, I'm in the same place.
When things don't function as I want them to.
I find it easy to point out at you -
Yet I'm quite certain this method's not right -
'Cause it so often leads into a fight.
I guess if I were just as smart as could be
I'd more often point my own finger at me.
If honesty reigned then the truth would be known—
Most problems I face are really my own.
To point out at you and to see you at fault
Could well end up in a massive assault—
Stir up more trouble than's already there
Then everyone loses and that's just not fair.
Because most things generally start out with me—
The more I look in the more likely I'll see
Answers which could help ease some of my pain—
Then I'd be happy and healthy, again.
Now we have finished our short little song
And if we follow, we'll seldom go wrong.
When we see things which are going awry
We need to stop and ask: "Lord, is it I?"

—Written by C. Beckert

Know Our Limits (15)

One major cause of imbalance is our inability and or unwillingness to recognize and remain within our limits. Everyone has limits. Continually exceeding our limits not only leaves us uncomfortable and out of balance but can actually kill us. Pace, rhythm, and tempo are the components of the hooping skill of cadence; understanding and respecting these components are critical.

We cannot be all things to all people nor can we be in two or more places at the same time. Intellectually we recognize this, but despite this knowledge many continue to live a life out of balance and beyond reasonable limits.

Remaining within limits and enjoying balance requires us to challenge unrealistic expectations—those we have for ourselves and those others have for us. We must recognize and work with those elements that are within our personal circle of control, while discarding and ignoring elements that are outside that circle. We can remain in balance when we assume responsibility only for those elements within our control area. Attempting to do otherwise invites frustration and disaster. Trying to control elements that are not ours to control is an exercise in futility.

Perhaps the best way to avoid stepping outside our limits is to learn to say "No!" And we don't have to justify and explain everything to others, either! Janet used this strategy. Somehow she needed to recognize and understand her limits. Unless she did, she would likely end up accomplishing less than what she could and pleasing fewer members of her family than she wanted to. She would also develop guilt feelings for not being able to do what she had agreed to do.

If we genuinely desire to regain and maintain balance, we must not stray from our limits. We understand the need to stretch to encourage personal growth, but such stretching should be reasonable or it will prove counterproductive. Sometimes we just need to say, "No, thank you. I know my limits!"

Listen to Your Body (16)

The human body has been called God's greatest miracle, and the human brain the finest piece of mechanism in the universe. We must learn to listen to what our body might tell us about our current condition.

The hooping skill of coordination provides the basis for this strategy. We must learn to coordinate what our body tells us with the choices we make if we want to maintain balance. One of the miracles of the human body is its ability to communicate with us and keep us updated about what is going on inside. Our bodies can tell us many things if we listen. They warn us of pending dangers, remind us of our need for food and water, and let us know when we are not feeling well, both physically and emotionally.

When we are out of balance, our bodies will likely feel it even before our minds recognize it. We can more easily maintain our balance if we listen to the signals our body sends out.

An example of this can be shown in this somewhat basic analogy (we hope this is not offensive). Have you ever wondered why most adolescents and adults avoid wetting their pants while infants and toddlers do not? It seems that the key is recognizing the need to go to the bathroom in time to take care of it, a simple message our bodies send us. Little ones have not yet learned to recognize and read these physical signals and do not become aware of their bathroom needs until they feel moisture. On the other hand, we have learned to recognize the body's signals indicating our need for a restroom.

Interestingly enough, different individuals sense this need in various ways indicating that not everyone experiences the same sensations in the same place and in the same way. Regardless of how the message is sent, we learn to recognize it and do whatever it takes to relieve the discomfort.

Remember thirteen-year-old David, who had a difficult time controlling his temper? He demonstrated acceptable self-control in some situations but lost control completely in others. One of the things DB tried to teach him was to listen to his body and catch himself before the anger took over. DB suggested he watch for sweaty hands, shaking knees, pressure in his head, or clenched fists, each of which may indicate that he was becoming frustrated. DB encouraged him to walk away or do something that would help him calm down when he noticed any of these reactions.

This idea of recognizing the physical signs or messages from our body works with adults as well and in a variety of circumstances other than anger management. Although the physical signs of being extremely anxious or angry are more common, such signs can also be experienced when we are overly excited or happy. We may laugh uncontrollably or tears of joy may flow down our cheeks. If we are extremely dependent on another individual, we may sense a tensing of our muscles or a constricting of our chest when we can't stay close to that person. The drumming of our fingers or the tapping of our toes may also be indicators of our unbalance.

Our bodies communicate with us about other matters as well. When we are out of balance, we generally sense it somewhere in our bodies. It may be in our stomach, throat, head, or hands and fingers. In fact, we could feel it in any one or more of these locations. When the body experience unbalance, it sends out distress signals. On the other hand, the closer we come to regaining balance, the less discomfort our body feels.

How does your body let you know something is out of balance? Learn to identify your body's communication style, and when unbalance is indicated, move in the direction needed to ease the discomfort and regain balance.

My Circle of Control (17)

One of the last things CB's mother said to him before she passed away was thanks for sharing the concept of the circle of control. This strategy helped her considerably during many stormy times in her life. She mentioned that until she recognized and accepted this idea, she had felt responsible for everything that happened to her. CB was grateful that her acceptance of this strategy had proven beneficial to her.

The circle of control concept suggests the existence of three concentric circles, beginning with a relatively small one in the center, with the other two circles increasing in size.

The larger, outer circle is labeled "Circle of Concern" and in it falls all situations and conditions in the world about which we are concerned but are rarely able to influence. In fact, we can only do two things about these concerns: we can pray about them, and in some instances, we can send money. In these instances, we do not have direct contact with the people involved or with the conditions that exist. But we can have concern for them.

The middle circle is labeled "Circle of Influence." Within this area are all situations on which we can exert influence. This circle includes people with whom we have contact in any way, shape, or form. For example, if we have written a book, we would have some influence on anyone reading our words.

Generally, we ourselves are influenced by those we might influence. In other words, individuals usually exist within each other's circle of influence. A teacher can certainly influence students, who in turn influence the teacher. If we are to maintain balance, we must recognize those circumstances where we have influence and those where we can only manifest concern.

The center and smallest circle is our "Circle of Control." This area contains circumstances over which we should have control. This circle is so small in comparison with the other two because there are relatively few areas of our lives that fall in this circle. Residing in this circle are *our* thoughts, *our* feelings, *our* actions, and *our* perceptions. Any thoughts, feelings, actions, and perceptions belonging to other people are not in this circle and must be accepted as part of the outer two circles.

Acceptance of this concept is vital for balance. Any time we attempt to control things outside of our circle of control, we are in danger of losing our balance because we are expending our time and energy not in our power to change. You can easily imagine how frustrating this could be.

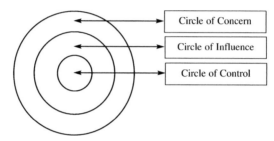

Understanding and accepting this concept should help us relax and enjoy life more, knowing we are not responsible for what others think, feel, or do. Of course, we have a responsibility to influence others in a positive way whenever possible, but we are not responsible for their decisions.

If you are feeling out of balance in a particular area of your life, analyze the situation and determine which problems and concerns are actually yours. Any attempt on your part to exert control over things outside your circle of control will likely result in frustration and discouragement, which are two of the most common consequences of being out of balance. As simple as this method appears, it is often difficult to apply because of the numerous pressures we feel within our culture.

Of the five hula hooping skills, control may have the broadest application; it is a central key to a life of balance and harmony.

My Preferred Personal Profile (18)

Writing something on paper has a significantly stronger impact on us than merely thinking or pondering about it. Putting our thoughts and dreams in writing requires analyzing, and it is generally well worth the extra effort. We have worked with individuals who were significantly out of balance and yet seemed oblivious to the pain and confusion they were experiencing. More than once people have observed that they actually felt better *before* they started therapy than they felt during therapy.

This is a common phenomenon. It is like learning to play a musical instrument. Generally, the beginning stages of learning are the most uncomfortable and most frustrating; they also require the most effort. However, once you have mastered a musical instrument, you can enjoy the benefits derived from putting in that beginning effort. Often, initial discomfort is critical to provide the motivation to change.

Writing a personal profile can be extremely effective in becoming aware of unbalance. However, this strategy should not be confused with the "Act As If" process described earlier. The only action required for this strategy is the actual writing of the description and not the acting it out.

This process works as follows:

Select several significant areas of your life with which you are less than totally satisfied. For example, start by asking yourself questions like these:

- How do I respond to others?
- How do I accomplish important tasks?
- Why does everything have to be perfect before I am content?
- How I am unable to share my feelings with my partner?

The answers to these questions will help you identify the areas in which you are not satisfied. You could ask yourself more questions, but if you ask too many, your list may be too lengthy.

Once you have listed the areas of your life with which you are unhappy, write a rather detailed description of each area, including where you are now in that area and where you would like to be. Your description should be reasonable, and you should not expect too much, too soon. Many who have used this strategy report that the realization of their problem and the motivation for change occurred simultaneously with the writing. They began to see, almost immediately, whether they were too far to the left or too far to the right regarding a particular character trait. Consequently, they quickly began to plan a way back to better balance.

Jeff might benefit significantly from this exercise. He was motivated to change and mainly needed direction. Once Jeff had completed his preferred profile, he would likely recognize how much he had already accomplished and perhaps give himself credit for goals he had already reached.

This strategy is especially effective if you are realistic and not prone to flights of fancy. However, it can cause additional problems if you describe yourself or how you want to see yourself in an exaggerated fashion, setting an ideal that is too difficult to reach. In most cases, however, this simple technique is more powerful than you might initially think. Give it a try, and you'll be surprised with the insightful personal information you discover.

Needs versus Wants (19)

Not long ago, CB mentioned to a patient that a major cause of the pressure the patient was feeling stemmed from the fact that he and his wife were confusing wants with needs. Frank, the patient, seemed taken aback by this suggestion, restating how important each of the stress-causing elements he had identified in his life was. In his mind, there was no realistic way to eliminate or even diminish his current load.

As we talked, it became more and more clear to both of us how items that had once been on a want list had now moved into the needs category. When this happens, wants are no longer optional but become mandatory. With this comes accompanying pressure.

In this particular instance, Frank had taken a part-time job in order to have "fun money," as he and his wife called it, so they could go on tours, take more elaborate vacations, and purchase nicer clothes. Frank insisted that these things were simply wants, and if they didn't materialize, no lasting discomfort would be felt.

With a tidy sum of fun money in their account, Frank and his wife began to think about remodeling their home. As it turned out, their expansion plans would take all of their savings account and then some, but they were confident they could pay off the loan in a year or so *with the part time job continuing*. Believing they could handle additional debt, they expanded their living space, made their home much more attractive and comfortable, and racked up debt reaching over $10,000. At that moment, their wants for discretionary items became a need in order to make the payments on their remodeling project. As a direct result of this change, working at the part-time job was no longer an option. Frank now had to work, whether or not he wanted to. Frank and his wife felt out of balance but couldn't understand what had happened. Had they clearly understood the consequences of so many needs, their lives would have been better balanced.

This strategy for regaining balance is a relatively simple paper-and-pencil exercise. Create a list of all the elements of your life that currently require time, money, and energy. This list does not have to be in any particular order at this time.

Once you've created the list, review it, and place an "N" (for need) or a "W" (for want) in front of each entry. Needs are items that are essential to sustain life, not lifestyle. Wants are elements that are nice but not necessary, meaning that if you didn't have these items or complete these functions, life would continue and no major pain or discomfort would be felt. You may miss these things, but they are expendable.

Now you have two lists, one of needs and one of wants. Now rank each item on the needs list in order of importance. You have already indicated that each one is important; that is why they appear on the needs list. However, prioritizing them provides you with greater insight about how to take care of them.

Now, do the same with your list of wants. This helps you obtain your most desired wants first.

You will be impressed with the balance you can obtain and maintain by separating your wants from your needs, and focusing your energy on what is most important.

As an aside, Frank and his wife decided life was too short to have so many needs. They sold their remodeled home within a year, moved into a smaller, less expensive one, worked at the part-time job once in a while, and enjoyed life a whole lot more. They had made the trip back from the out-of-balance world and loved it.

This strategy can also help individuals who make inappropriate and ineffective decisions in an attempt to fulfill what they consider a need, when in reality what they are seeking is only a want.

This was the situation with Joan, who felt she had to please others in order to be liked. To be liked by others is more of a want than a need. Had Joan realized this, she could have avoided many of her most uncomfortable feelings, which resulted from choosing wrongly to please others.

If you choose to implement this strategy, you must take the time to consider the things you want most. Unless you do this, this strategy will not work.

Outside My Comfort Zone (20)

In trying to regain or maintain balance we are likely going to experience genuine discomfort. Understandably, most of us are afraid to take any risks that might nudge us out of our comfort (though not so comfortable) zones. However, unless we are willing to take risks, we will unlikely return to a state of balance.

Many of us are afraid of change, afraid of trying something strange and new. But, unless we are willing to challenge our current situation and condition, we retard our personal growth and remain where we are, out of balance.

On the other hand, it is generally unwise to attempt too big of a change at one time. While it is true that the higher the risk, the greater the returns, we need to also understand the opposite: the higher the risk, the greater the fall.

We suggest most patients make small, incremental changes rather than go all out. Knowing they only have to take a baby step instead of a giant step out of their comfort zone lessons most people's fears. Continuous changes can serve us well and transport us to a condition of better balance.

A word often used in connection with progression toward excellence is *stretching*. If we don't stretch, we won't progress. So go ahead. Think of something small that you can do or change and move forward. Stretch a little. Risk a little. Like the proverbial turtle, if we don't stick our neck out, it is unlikely we will move forward. Challenge your comfort zone, and return to balance and peace.

Suppose you are trying to overcome feelings of superiority. One small step might be to allow others to make the final comment during conversations. Suppress your desire to have the last word. Maybe you'd ask a friend's opinion about something, then listen carefully to what he or she has to say. Don't forget to thank him or her for the contribution.

Many individuals who are out of balance on the superior side have the tendency to talk loud. A small step may be to talk in a quieter voice with a gentler tone. These small, specific "stretches" will assist a return to balance.

Putting Things into Perspective (21)

Do you remember the first time you discovered that binoculars could either bring things closer or push them farther in the distance? So it is with life. We can bring things into focus and ourselves into balance by altering our perspective through looking at our situations and ourselves in different ways.

Many times it is as simple as asking yourself, "How important will this situation be in twenty years?" While the situation doesn't change, our answer to that question often changes our perspective. Being willing and able to look at the bigger picture benefits most of us. However, it is much like putting a jigsaw puzzle together: trying to find the correct place for each puzzle piece is much more difficult when we cannot see what the completed puzzle looks like.

Another area where perspective is extremely important is temporality, or time. Our sense of unbalance often results from not understanding the relationship between the past, the present, and the future. If our focus remains on only one of these areas, life becomes too complex to understand. We should try to view life in relationship to all three time periods because they are so interconnected. In fact, they are not only defined by each other but exist only in relationship to each other. What seems too monumental in the present moment may be much less ominous after a good night's sleep. How many times have we awakened in the morning either very happy or very unhappy about how we handled a situation the day before?

There is a story about Tug McGraw, a star relief pitcher for the New York Mets around 1960. He was called into the game in the final innings, generally with the game on the line, to secure the final outs and save the win. What pressure he must have felt!

One day a reporter asked him how he handled these day-to-day pressures so well. Tug McGraw's answer went something like this: "I just think about the future and how much my effort will mean fifty years from now, and then things do not seem so critical."

We can all learn from those words. When we sense an unbalance in our lives, we need to take the time, find a way, and make the effort to put the incident, thought, or feeling into proper perspective.

Recognize An Opinion for What It Is—An Opinion (22)

We often see people who have been sent to us by their spouse to be "fixed." In the opinion of the person doing the sending, our patient is broken, out of balance, and in need of repair. Often, this is not the case. However, the attitude of the "sending" spouse indicates a deeper relationship problem.

If someone is told often enough that he is broken in some way, he will begin to believe it. And once something is believed strongly enough, it will generally be acted out.

This cycle suggests the possibility that a person may feel out of balance when, in reality, he is not. So we see the importance of listening to feedback from others but recognizing it as an *opinion* and not necessarily truth. While it may be true, just because someone says it doesn't make it so.

We help people understand this strategy by having them label the information they receive from others with an "(insert initial) O." For example, if your friend Mary says you need to loosen up about housecleaning, you would label what she shares with you as "MO," or Mary's Opinion. This doesn't mean that you don't listen to what she says. It means that you understand and accept the statement for what it is—someone's opinion based upon how they view the situation. Of course, the more significant the sharing person is in our lives, the more value we give to their opinions.

As you receive and evaluate opinions, ask yourself this key question: Is there any truth to this opinion? If you feel there may be some truth to the opinion, you can accept it and make whatever changes in your attitudes or behaviors that you see fit.

If, on the other hand, you feel the opinion is not true, you don't need to argue with the person sharing the opinion. Remember that the information is just an opinion, and he has the right to think what he will—you just don't have to act upon it!

You might also ask this question: What have I done or not done that has given this person this perception of me? If you don't know the answer, you might ask the person sharing the opinion. Regardless, whether you act on the opinion is your choice.

The main thing we want to do is learn what we need to learn and subsequently do what we need to do to return balance in our lives, remembering that opinions are just that, opinions! We should listen to them and carefully decide if we will act on it.

Recognizing Our Self-Worth (23)

Few strategies help us regain and maintain balance more quickly than this one. The premise for this strategy is that when we realize and accept our unconditional and personal worth, we seek a condition where we feel most comfortable. Such a place would be where we do not have to be anything we are not or do anything we do not desire to do. Simply stated, we do not need to go to any extreme to experience the love and acceptance we desire.

When we feel good about ourselves, we realize that no person or situation can make us less than we are. We not only feel more comfortable when we accept our intrinsic worth, but we also sense control over our lives. As individuals of unconditional worth and value, we deserve to experience peace and harmony—and we can.

Interestingly enough, this concept is more easily understood and accepted by adults than by teens. We try to counsel younger patients, such as David, in a direction where they can experience the feeling of someone considering them to be worthwhile. While this is easier said than done, it can be done.

We must understand this concept. Let's say, for example, that you have a special gift of performing surgery. Is your self-worth based on your special talents? What if you are involved in a car accident in which your hands are permanently disabled? This obviously affects your ability to perform surgery, but does that mean you are without worth?

Absolutely not! Although it alters your ability to do certain things, it does not alter your basic self-worth. We all have value and worth regardless of any talents, skills, gifts, or abilities. We simply inherit our self-worth as a child of God.

We suggest our clients read—and re-read—the following self-worth statements:

- I am worthwhile, not for what I am, but because I am.
- I may not be perfect, but I am important.
- No matter what you say or do to me, I am still a worthwhile person.
- When I fail at a thing, I fail at a thing. I am not a failure.
- My challenge in life is not to be the best but to do my best.
- I act in a manner consistent with the way I see myself.
- I only feel a sense of inferiority in the presence of a comparison, which, at best, is inaccurate and unfair.
- To know me is to love me.
- We tend to move in the direction of our most dominant thought pattern.
- I will think in positive terms.

Many of our patients make it a daily ritual to read this entire list while others focus on one of the statements for a day or a week. The primary objective of these statements is to internalize how significant we are in our world. If you interpret this to mean that you should become proud, pompous, and conceited, then you are thinking in terms of extremes; this is not what we are suggesting.

Redefining Words and Phrases (24)

Many of us feel out of balance because we are trapped by the definitions and understandings we have of certain words and phrases. Some people are so imprisoned by this they are unable to change those definitions. The primary function of this strategy is to establish a sense of freedom that enables a person to view what he is experiencing from another perspective.

Take for an example the word *perfection*. Because the concept of perfection suggests something or someone without the slightest flaw, it looms as an impossibility to ever achieve. Yet many view it as a commandment. Our strategy of focus suggests that we put a slightly different spin on the word.

Putting a little different spin on the word *be* also helps. We suggest that you change the word, in some instances, to *become,* which represents a process rather than a state of being. It relieves a great amount of pressure to believe we are to *become* perfect rather than *be* perfect. After all, each of us can be realistically considered a work in progress.

When we view perfection as a process rather than an event, we do not feel trapped. In addition, when we view perfection in periods of time shorter than eternity, we also feel less restricted. An example of this may be realizing that *today* I have been perfect in my challenge to not use profanity or not overeat. To be perfect in an area of life for a day is certainly more feasible than to define perfection only in terms of forever.

We have also suggested that our patients substitute the word *excellence* for *perfection*, thereby providing them with a greater sense of freedom. In most of our minds, to strive for excellence is more motivating than to strive to be without a flaw. This strategy would work extremely well with someone like Jane, whose frustration was primarily due to her belief that those around her expected her to be perfect.

Not long ago a couple came into the office to discuss the behavior of some of their children. The father was out of balance because he was attempting to force his children to obey and was not being success-ful. Can you see the irony of that? Obedience cannot be forced! When obedient behavior is forced, it is compliance, not obedience. One can force compliance but never obedience. Obedience requires freedom of choice.

No wonder two of their children were in open rebellion, and the father felt out of control and balance. The children were being required to choose freely, and that just cannot be done. Once the father redefined his understanding of the word *obedience*, he realized he had been expecting the impossible. He mellowed and asked for assistance in teaching him how to *encourage* his children to obey. Obedience, not compliance, is the first law of heaven.

There are other common words that are often misinterpreted. When we confuse these words, we end up out of balance. Those words include:

- *Attending* confused with *participating*
- *Reading* confused with *understanding*
- *Listening* confused with *hearing*
- *Intimacy* confused with *sex*
- *Looking* confused with *seeing*
- *Activity* confused with *production*
- *Talking* confused with *communicating*
- *Saying* confused with *believing*
- *Involvement* confused with *presence*
- *Expedience* confused with *correctness*
- *Efficiency* confused with *effectiveness*
- *Urgency* confused with *importance*

A skilled baseball pitcher can make a ball move in many different ways depending on the spin he puts on the ball. So it is with words and phrases. The way we define and understand them determines the direc-tion we will go in response to them. Redefining words and phrases can be a powerful vehicle to transport us back into balance.

Release Your Brakes (25)

Have you ever wondered why you are unable to accomplish some-thing, even though you know that if you did you would feel much more in balance and less stressed? You're not alone! Most of us have wanted to do something or to go somewhere in the worst way, but for some reason or another, we just can't seem to get there.

The majority of people who find themselves in this situation honestly believe the solution is trying even harder to move things along. We have labeled this effort "more of the same." Frustration is seldom eased by the will power to succeed.

The focus of this balancing technique is not on trying harder but on removing whatever is blocking our progress and ultimate success. Let's suppose you are in a stopped car, but you'd like to move forward. You step on the gas pedal, but the car doesn't move. You step on the gas a little harder or a little longer, but again, the car refuses to move.

After a little investigation, you discover that the problem is not with the gas pedal but with the brake pedal. You realize that your left foot is on the brake, and no matter how hard you press down on the gas pedal, the brake keeps you solidly in place. The key is to remove your left foot from the brake, and then the car will move.

So it is with life. So many times we want to go forward but are unable to move. Simply trying harder is not the answer. Instead, we need to find out what might be blocking our progress or what barriers we are facing.

In the case of Mitchell and Sandi, they were determined to make things right and felt they could do so by just trying harder. In their situation, the harder they tried to *make* things better, the worse things became. They needed to discover and discard the attitudes and behaviors that were blocking their improvement.

In the struggle to return to balance, we would like to suggest what might seem like an odd procedure. Most people approach life in this pattern: determine goal > perform actions required > achieve goal. We suggest this pattern instead: determine goal > identify barriers between us and our goal > determine how to overcome each barrier > implement the means > move toward the goal.

For example, let's say we want to hold a regular family meeting. Although we have tried many different things, we still struggle to meet together on a weekly basis as a family. Here is how our "Release Your Brakes" strategy might help find the balance we seek as a family relative to providing a time and a place to consider and make necessary adjustments in our family life.

GOAL: To hold a regular and effective family meeting each week.

Barriers	Means to Overcome Barriers
Too many good TV programs on	Good use of your VCR
Too much effort and energy needed	Learn to delegate duties and share responsibilities
Children don't want to attend	Involve family members in the planning Teach on their level Shorten the experience Start and stop on time
Monday is a bad day	Shift days
Everyone is too busy	Schedule as a family Hold a meeting regularly so all can get used to it Hold it even if someone cannot attend

Releasing your brakes will assist many in returning to balance in their lives.

Successive Approximations (26)

A speaker in a psychology class once introduced his lecture with this one-liner: "Folks, psychology is a science where you are told something you already know in a language you can't understand." After sitting through his introductory lecture, CB realized how truthful he had been and wondered if he had really meant it as a joke!

One of his hard-to-understand concepts, which actually represented a simple and well-known truth, was successive approximations. To approximate something means to come closer to it. Successive suggests our movement toward our goal be gradual, one foot in front of the other.

The primary reason this strategy works is that we experience success with each small step in the desired direction, thus maintaining an even stronger motivation because of repeated successes. The saying "Success breeds success" is true, and it stands to reason that if we can experience success more immediately and frequently, the more willing we will be to continue our progress toward balance.

These two popular sayings describe this strategy.

- How do you eat an elephant? One bite at a time.
- A journey of a thousand miles begins with a single step.

If Betty had felt that her husband, Brent, supported her in a gradual weight-loss program, she might have been more motivated to do what was needed to lose the extra pounds, but she did not have this feeling. In her mind, Brent would only be satisfied when all the excess weight was gone. The thought of losing so much weight so quickly was very discouraging, so Betty finally chose to not try.

An example of this strategy at work is Mary Ann. Mary Ann had a weight problem and had battled her weight for many years. She had high blood pressure and high cholesterol. Although she had tried several diet programs, none of them clicked with her. During a routine physical examination, her doctor requested a blood sugar test, the results of which added Type II diabetes to her list of health problems.

This news shocked Mary Ann, and she feared for her future. The thought of losing over fifty pounds overwhelmed her, and she felt doomed to failure before she even started. But she was motivated and came in the office to talk about what she might do. We outlined an eating plan and, key to her success, changed the goal of losing fifty pounds to a goal of losing one to two pounds a week. The eating regime, the attainable goal, and the motivation—even though it was based on fear—were enough to encourage Mary Ann to move forward. And move forward she did—one pound at a time.

Applying this principle when we are out of balance suggests we decide where we would like to be and then identify several smaller goals, each representing a move closer to our final goal. Remember the skill of cadence, pace, tempo and rhythm? This plan will work; try it.

The Right Thing for the Right Reason (Where Is Your heart?) (27)

CB remembers a telephone call from Sam, who said he was extremely desperate and needed to talk with someone as quickly as possible. There was something about the call that confused CB: although Sam's words indicated desperation, his voice and tone did not.

When CB met Sam in the office later that week, his suspicions were confirmed Sam was an extremely manipulative individual. Everything with Sam had an angle, which always pointed in his direction. He wasn't as desperate as he had indicated. He *was* confused and frustrated because he was no longer able to manipulate his wife the way he had been doing for so many years.

His initial comments went something like this: "I don't understand her anymore. Nothing I do appears to make a difference, and no matter how hard I try, she won't budge and let me back into her life. I buy her gifts, I provide more money than the court requires, I mow the lawn and do the yard work, but nothing works." Then he said what I had expected. "I've got to convince her to take me back, or I will lose my business and everything I've worked for."

It was no wonder Sam's "system" didn't work. He was doing good things for his wife, but his motives were totally selfish, and his wife apparently saw through his whole charade. Our motives for doing something are often more important than what we do. Doing the right things for the wrong reasons is not much better than having good intentions but not putting them into action.

This technique for regaining balance suggests two things: one, take a close look at what you are doing to make things better, and two, make certain your motives are pure and unselfish. You can find peace and harmony in the service of others—if your motives are pure.

Visualize and Simulate (28)

Many individuals have used the strategy of visualization in numerous situations and circumstances. Visualization involves seeing yourself actually doing what you want to accomplish, whether it is refusing that second piece of cake, going to a dance without the aid of alcohol, or jumping over the bar in the high jump event of a track meet. Some promoters of positive thinking state that we can achieve whatever we can perceive.

This strategy is often used to great advantage in athletic endeavors.

Golfers visualize their putt trailing directly to the hole and then dropping in. Place kickers see, in their mind's eye, the football sailing end over end through the goal posts. Competitive divers go over in their minds every minute detail of their upcoming dives. The examples are endless.

Similar results can be experienced when a yelling father visualizes himself coming home to an unacceptable situation and calmly expressing his feelings about what has happened. He sees himself opening the door and closing it with gentleness. He sees himself giving his children a gentle hug rather than yelling at them. As he visualizes his altered behavior, he senses the peace and harmony that come with his new actions.

Another example of this strategy may be a busy mother visualizing herself answering the telephone and saying "no." If she can see herself doing it in her mind, there is a much better chance of her doing it in real life!

When it comes to gaining or maintaining balance, this strategy may be one of the most productive. Take Matthew for instance. Had Matthew been able to visualize himself connecting with his wife, the chances of them actually connecting would have increased. And had they been able to connect on a consistent basis, they may have avoided a divorce.

The effects of emotional visualization are surprisingly strong. Many studies indicate that our emotional reaction to a visualized experience is identical to the emotional reactions we would exhibit in an actual circumstance.

Picture yourself enjoying peace and harmony, whatever scenes that thought might bring to your mind, and you will be experiencing balance. It's wonderful, isn't it?

Walk Away (29)

Over the years, we have counseled hundreds of individuals whose lives were out of balance due to a personal habit or pattern of behavior that was not in line with the way they wanted to live their lives. They could not enjoy personal peace and harmony as long as this behavior persisted. What they wanted from us, as therapists, was to find ways to eliminate the self-defeating behavior they were involved in. Examples of self-defeating actions include overeating, pornography, self-abuse, angry outbursts, profanity, gossiping, excessive teasing, and so on.

The longer people allow themselves to stay in temptation's way of these self-defeating behaviors, the more likely they are to lose their balance. Take, for example, those who struggle with overeating. The longer they stand in front of an open refrigerator door telling themselves they shouldn't eat anything, the more likely they will put something in their mouth. Or, when someone battling pornography sees a questionable image on the computer or TV screen and continues to look at it rather than looking away or changing the channel, he is reinforcing the destructive habit.

We often teach this three-step pattern to immoral actions: First, we look, then we linger, and then we lust. When you change the word *lust* to *give in,* the concept applies to any number of problematic behaviors. By remaining in stressful or tempting situations, we increase the probability of giving in to established patterns and losing our balance.

To combat this, we teach a simple, two-word process—walk away! Physically remove yourself from the unbalancing situation or circumstance, and walk or even run to another place. Whether we are in a tempting situation, or sense our anger reaching a boiling point, or are with people who are talking about others inappropriately, or in a theater viewing violent or sexual scenes we don't want to see, we generally have the power to walk away. When we do so, we maintain our balance and avoid the discomfort that comes from doing something we don't want to do. And if we are in a circumstance where we cannot physically walk away, we may be able to do so in our minds by concentrating on another situation that is acceptable. Walking away can be a tremendous help in obtaining and sustaining equilibrium.

Why Should I Do It? (30)

One lesson we have learned is that nobody does anything unless there is something in it for him. We realize this sounds too general to be true, but think about it. Other than our automatic reflexes, everything we do, we do for a reason, to get something, reach something, eliminate something, or avoid something.

There are all types of rewards in this world that motivate us. Sometimes the reward is not something we receive but rather avoiding a punishment, which in itself is a reward. Rewards can be tangible items, such as money, food, or material goods. Rewards can also be intangible items, such as fame, prestige, or even that "good feeling" deep inside.

For example, Brent had a definite, positive reversal of his attitude toward his wife's weight, but only after he realized what he would lose if she chose to leave him. Brent made significant changes because he didn't want to lose his wife. In this regard, adults are no different than adolescents, although adults seem better able to distinguish between worldly treasures (extrinsic rewards) and spiritual treasures (intrinsic rewards) a little more effectively.

This strategy maintains that when we find ourselves out of balance and wanting to return to balance, a change in our thinking and behavior is mandated. Such a change generally requires effort, sometimes a lot, and other times a little.

Many individuals find it helpful to visualize the rewards, real or fancied, which await them once they return to balance. One of the rewards for not gossiping about your friend is the way you will feel the next time you meet her. You won't want to avoid her and cross to the other side of the street to avoid the meeting. If we want what we visualize badly enough, we will be more than willing to expend the time and energy required to make whatever change is indicated.

The real keys are to know the answer to the question, "What's in it for me?" and to desire the potential reward. Then we must put into action what we have learned.

The Use of Prescription Medication (31)

We'd like to include a brief statement regarding the use of prescriptive medications in assisting individuals to reach peace and harmony in their lives. As a psychiatrist and a psychologist, we have seen the value that medication and modern science produce. We are also aware of the many abuses of medication. We feel it is extremely important to know when and what medications are used.

Human nature tends to take the route of least resistance when it comes to reducing physical and emotional discomfort and pain, and so many turn to medication. Medication generally acts more quickly than psychotherapy in reducing our distress. Practioners desirous of helping their patients are at times pressured into prescribing medications prematurely.

We support the use of medications but do so with a conservative perspective. We would like to suggest the following guiding principles for those who choose to use medication as a means to personal balance.

First and foremost, the doctor and patient should determine the root cause of the problem rather than simply treating the symptoms. Too often we see individuals thinking and acting in unhealthy ways, who turn to a medication to solve their problems rather than altering their behavior.

For example, as mental health professionals, we encounter people who are depressed. In their efforts to ease their suffering, they seek a "magic" pill. If, however, the depression is the result of low self-esteem or poor choices, medications only temporarily mask or hide the discomfort.

Ponder the following illustration: The root cause of Emily's discomfort is low self-esteem. The symptoms we see include depression, anxiety, anger, doubt, frustration, and the avoidance of uncomfortable situations. As good and progressive as medicine is, there is not, and presumably never will be, an anti-doubt or anti-frustration pill.

Rather, the root of the problem must be treated through therapy, and although medications can moderate the depressive, anxious, anger, or frustration symptoms, they can never completely resolve them. We do on occasion prescribe medications to assist patients and their spouses, families, and friends to be more comfortable while they develop and make the necessary changes in thoughts, words, and behaviors, but it is only a secondary means of helping. The intent of medication is to lessen the emotional pain and suffering without striping the individual of the motivation to change. Overcoming unhealthy thoughts and behaviors can lead to self-mastery, independence, peace, contentment, harmony, and balance.

Despite this strategy, we do suggest the following general priorities: 1) If possible, avoid the use of medications. Often we see individuals who find medications helpful enough that it takes pain away, which is often the motivation for change. As a result, many patients use medications as a crutch instead of finding the real cause of the behavior they want to change. They never get better. 2) If medications are indicated, use them temporarily while those involved develop healthier ways to address the root problem. 3) If medications are necessary as an integral method of treatment for a chemical unbalance or a genetic predisposition, learn about the possible side effects and work closely with your physician.

Medication can serve a purpose, especially for the treatment of *severe* unbalance. Keep in mind the following:

1) Medication is an accepted treatment of choice for significant loss of functioning (e.g., depression) or genetically involved mental illness (e.g., schizophrenia). The more significant a person's illness or inability to function, the more aggressive and intensive the treatment must be. This suggests that if an individual is considering suicide or is not eating, sleeping,

concentrating, bathing, or going to work, the use of medications, hospitalization, or other measures must be considered.

2) Medications may be necessary to assist young children who do not have the maturity or coping strategies to handle their disability (e.g., attention deficit hyperactivity disorder [ADHD]). For example, a six-year-old child who suffers from ADHD with the combination of hyperactivity and inattention can be severely affected in his academic and social functioning.

Children are not always motivated to make adjustments in their lives because they do not recognize they are developing their academic foundation for their schooling and life's work. Their immediate focus is on what they are having for lunch or who they can play with during recess. Medication can help these children reach their academic and social potential.

3) Medications should generally be considered to ameliorate symptoms that interfere with the progress of talk therapy treatment.

We support the use of medications in treating those suffering from the effects of emotional distress. But we also warn against the use of medications to treat symptoms without addressing the root cause of the difficulty. It is wise to begin any therapy with the least intrusive treatment and increase the intensity as the situation warrants. It is paramount to seek competent professional assistance from someone who has the required training and experience to administer appropriate medication.

Notes

1. Harold S. Kushner, *When Bad Things Happen to Good People* (New York: Avon, 1997).

2. Marvin J. Ashton, Area Director's Convention, LDS Church Office Building, Salt Lake City, Utah, March 31, 1982.

Section V
Summary and Conclusions

In our many years of practice, we have worked with numerous individuals, couples, families, and groups in a variety of situations. Our training and experience also include working with children, adolescents, and adults involved in the private, public, and criminal-justice systems. As a result, we have seen and treated a diverse collection of problems with every conceivable combination and blend of situations, severity, and frequency. We have also become painfully and clearly aware of common threads woven throughout these difficulties. Although people and their problems differ widely, we see universal barriers that crop up preventing people from attaining their full potential.

Many of these challenges are complex and intricate. However, most problems can generally be categorized into one of three major areas of unbalance: genetics, temperament, or environment.

Genetics: Mental health research is progressing at an astounding rate. Current research indicates that many illnesses are strongly impacted or even caused by genetic factors. For example, alcohol and drug addiction, certain anxiety disorders (e.g., obsessive compulsive disorder, schizophrenia, bipolar affective disorder, and depression) are heavily influenced by genetics. Just as our hair or eye color, height, or looks are derived from our parents, genetic loading produces many mental health illnesses. Genetics can and do affect balance.

Temperament: We are all born with a certain personality makeup. Any parent who has more than one child recognizes that each child brings with him a specific set of personality traits. While one child may be quiet and reserved, a sibling is inquisitive and active. These multiple and varied features bring variety and zest to humanity.

However, along with positive characteristics come negative aspects. For instance, an individual may be extremely organized in his thinking and behavior almost from birth, which is generally viewed as a positive trait by society. However, when taken to an extreme, this tendency often results in an inflexibility that creates difficulties for both the individual and those with whom they work and live.

Environment: Given our individual combinations of genetics and temperament, we can be further influenced and affected by environmental factors, such as birth order, number of children in the family, parenting styles, religious orientation, socioeconomic factors, health of an individual or family member, influence of friends, educational level, and individual experiences including physical abuse and teasing by peers, etc.

For example, an individual raised in a strict, inflexible environment where individual thoughts were stifled and physical aggression was witnessed will have different experiences than someone raised in a more nurturing environment where humor, fun, and individuality were appreciated and fostered.

Even individuals within the same family have different reactions to the same environment. Some people are more "hardy" and not only survive but also thrive under certain conditions, while others receive significant emotional injury from the same experiences.

One family comes to mind: The parents had six children, ranging in age from three to nine years of age, who were exposed to an extremely chaotic home environment. Both parents were heavily involved in the sale and use of illicit drugs, and the children were frequently exposed to unknown people passing in and out of the household at all hours. These children witnessed physical abuse, drug use, theft, and other terrible things to which no child should be exposed. Their parents were mostly emotionally and physically unavailable because of frequent trips to prison.

There were no consistent family rules, parental modeling, or emotional stability in the home. In spite of this dysfunctional early home life, one child excelled in all areas of her life. Three of the children were somewhat neutral and impartial in their responses to their horrific home life and performed adequately in both academic and social arenas. Two of the children were severely and negatively affected and will likely follow in their parents' footsteps. In truth, we anticipated all the children might have taken this route, so environmental factors can certainly be overcome!

Clearly, genetics, temperament, and environment can, in combination with one another, produce a wide variety of results. Yet, depending on the combination, length, and severity of these factors, outcomes can vary. We have focused primarily on the temperamental or characterlogical aspects of people's lives because these are most amenable to change and are generally within our control.

Frequently, we are asked if a person can change, and the answer is a resounding yes, especially if the difficulties an individual is facing result from an extreme character trait. We can control our views and responses to the world. It is extremes in these views and reactions that create unbalance. These extremes can be modified by the appropriate application of the principles of hula hooping and the five suggested "C" skills: coordination, concentration, control, cadence, and continuous motion.

We have seen firsthand the disharmony and pain resulting from extreme attitudes and behaviors. The pursuit of balance can bring peace and harmony into people's lives. Although this journey requires work, discomfort, and courage, the result is worth every ounce of time and energy spent in its pursuit.

We hope the options we offer here prove helpful in your quest for balance. We have seen, time and time again, people make tremendous changes in their lives when they are serious about changing and willing to do what it takes.

Where to Go from Here?

As a young man, DB attended a presentation given by a man he deeply respected. The man seemed consistently in balance with his thoughts and behaviors, and he lived a happy life. He was addressing the subject of overcoming difficult habits that control and enslave us, and in his remarks, he emphasize three main points.

- Start where you are. That doesn't sound too difficult; each of us can do that.
- Set goals and time frames to be successful. This gentleman suggested that we set attainable goals regardless of how simple the task or short the time interval may be. He also suggested changing parameters in order to experience success. If we can't do something for a day, we should try it for an hour. If an hour is too long, shoot for a minute.
- Never give up. This man emphasized that we should continue

to work at achieving our goal no matter how slow things seemed to go. This philosophy can prevent us from being overwhelmed as we struggle with different faults and weaknesses.

Mother Teresa inspired and motivated millions who met her or read about her. As a nun, she felt she had been called to provide for the sick, poor, and needy of India. On one occasion, a report apparently mentioned that regardless of what she did, many more individuals would never be helped. To this observation, Mother Teresa responded, "I can't do everything, but I can do something." We can all do something to become more balanced in our individual lives.

Let us begin today.

Note

1. M. Russell Ballard, "Keeping Life's Demands in Balance," *Ensign*, May 1987, 13.

Charles B. Beckert

Charles B. Beckert was born in Logan, Utah, the second of six children. His elementary school years were spent in Brigham City, Utah, and he graduated from Weber High School in Ogden, Utah. He was active in student government, music, and athletics during his high school years. Dr. Beckert filled an LDS Mission in Germany, and upon his return, he married Olga Boeslund in the Logan LDS Temple. They are approaching their forty-seventh wedding anniversary.

The Beckerts raised four sons and are grandparents to thirteen.

Dr. Beckert holds education degrees from Weber State College, Utah State University, and Brigham Young University where he completed his doctoral work, earning a PhD in marriage and family therapy. Dr. Beckert taught in the LDS Church Educational System for thirty-seven years and maintained a private practice as a certified psychologist and marriage and family therapist from 1974 to 2001.

He has published three books and fifteen audio tapes dealing primarily with psychological and family issues.

His personal (retirement) hobbies include wood carving, golf, playing guitar, and doing counted cross-stitch. He continues his involvement with church service.

Derry L. Brinley

Dr. Derry L. Brinley was born and raised in south Texas. He is the second of four children. He filled an LDS mission in Michigan and later graduated from Weber State University with a degree in biology and a double minor in chemistry and communications.

He attended and graduated from medical school at the University of Health Sciences and completed two years of a family practice residency at the University of Kansas. He later completed a psychiatry residency and a child and adolescent psychiatry fellowship at the University of Wisconsin–Madison.

Dr. Brinley has been in practice for the past twelve years. He currently divides his time between his private practice at the Southwest Behavioral Health Center in St. George, Utah, and inpatient hospital care.

He is the proud father of two children, Adam and Daniel. His greatest joy and pleasure is his association with family and friends. His favorite activities are to spend time with his friends and family, his church and community service, reading, learning, fishing, boating, hiking, wildlife observation, and other outdoor activities.